Married
to Baseball

Other books and writing by
SUZANNE MOLINO SINGLETON

Baltimore's Little Italy:
History and Heritage of The Neighborhood
(pen name: Suzanna Rosa Molino)
2015, The History Press, S.C.

Flying by the Seat of My Biking Pants:
Reflections on Life as we Pedal Along
2015

SNIPPETS inspiration
a weekly inspirational think-out-loud e-column (since 2006)
SNIPPETSinspiration.com

Editor, *Neighborhood News from Little Italy, Baltimore*
promotioncenterforlittleitaly.org

OUT OF PRINT TITLES

Clever Gift Giving

Clever Party Planning:
Parties for kids, teens and adults

Clever Costume Creating for Halloween:
An A to Z guide of 200 costume ideas

Married
to Baseball

Between innings with Ken Singleton

Mrs. Singy's stories of baseball life that have nothing – and everything – to do with the game

Suzanne Molino Singleton

Foreword by Ken Singleton

Copyright © 2016 by Suzanne Molino Singleton
All rights reserved.

ISBN-13: 978-1519264909; **ISBN-10:** 1519264909

PERMISSIONS

Some of the content contained herein originally appeared on YESNetwork.com and MLB.com in an official Major League Baseball blog written by Suzanne Molino Singleton, *Mrs. Singy: Married to Baseball* 2009-13, and is used with permission from YES Network (Yankees Entertainment & Sports), New York, N.Y.

The Baltimore Orioles, New York Yankees and YES Network have approved recurring use of their trademarks in some photos.

Cover photos courtesy: Baltimore Orioles, Cool Kids Campaign, New York Botanical Garden, E.H. Wallop/YES Network

SUMMARY

Emotional, humorous and entertaining sketches of baseball life that have nothing – and everything – to do with the game. Based on 2009-2013 official MLB blog posts from *Mrs. Singy: Married to Baseball* by Suzanne Molino Singleton (wife of Ken Singleton, New York Yankees TV broadcaster and retired Baltimore Oriole), the stories are stuffed with Ken's insight, memories and distinctive baseball perspective and expertise. Highlighted with the Singletons' personal photos, Mrs. Singy describes life between innings and through baseball's historical milestones, even a few out-in-left-field topics.

Cover Design

Linda Ports, LP Designs
Perry Hall, MD

Editing

Nancy Menefee Jackson, Gerry Jackson
Baltimore, MD

All rights reserved. No part of this book, including photos, may be reproduced or transmitted in any form whatsoever without prior written permission from the author, except in the case of brief quotations embodied in articles and reviews.

DEDICATION

To "Hubs," Kenneth Wayne Singleton,
with everlasting love in honor of our 25th wedding
anniversary, and in absolute awe of your
adoration and knowledge of baseball

To Ma & Pop Singy in heaven, we miss you daily. With eternal gratefulness for your sweet love, acceptance and support; and for producing such a gracious gentleman in your son "Kenny"

CONTENTS

4TH INNING

5TH INNING

6TH INNING

7TH INNING

8TH INNING

9TH INNING

"Mr. & Mrs. Singy"
Ken Singleton and
Suzanne Molino Singleton
(Photo courtesy New York Botanical Garden)

FOREWORD

By Ken Singleton

When Suzanne and I began dating, she soon realized how much the game of baseball was a major part of my life. Sure, she knew that I had been a popular player with her hometown Baltimore Orioles; as a fan, she had seen me play at Memorial Stadium on many occasions.

After I moved to the broadcast booth and a new career, she witnessed the amount of preparation necessary for each and every game I announce on television.

Suzanne has been listening to my baseball anecdotes being told over and over through 25 years of marriage and always has encouraged me to write a book. But she's the writer.

When she realized she had plenty of stories to call her own, she began to pen them, and was accepted in April 2009 as a columnist on the NY Yankees' YESNetwork.com where *Mrs. Singy: Married to Baseball* was very well received by fans. Her inspirational and entertaining tales describe what it's like "between innings."

My wife is a very special woman, able to take care of things at home while I'm on the road. I appreciate that Suzanne accepts, sometimes reluctantly, that I must travel and be away from our family quite often during the baseball season.

I love her dearly, even more so because she has been able to deal with the fact that she is not only married to me, but also married to baseball.

"Coming to the Orioles in 1977 already having four brothers, I never thought of having 25 more added to the family. The love we felt for each other and the game was learned in a fun and raging way that I will never forget ... I wouldn't change my 25 'brothers' for any other 25."

- Eddie Murray #33, retired Oriole

1ST INNING

The Players,
the Teammates
and a few Big Names

The Baltimore baseball bond

Major League Baseball has players changing teams more often than they change jockstraps. One week a player wears blue and white, the next he dons black and orange. One month he's in the National League; the next in the American. One year he rents a house in Baltimore, then California.

Seldom do players sit on the same bench for their entire career, form lifelong friendships with teammates, or anchor themselves in a city long enough to call it home.

Yet there was a time. In the 1970s and -'80s, the Baltimore Orioles were more than teammates wearing matching jerseys. They were community members, godparents to each other's kids, neighbors and friends sharing a common profession. They didn't just play baseball in Baltimore; they lived and socialized here, they made appearances and they supported the town.

These guys played in an era when Major Leaguers stayed put, performed for one team and formed attachments to each other in dugouts and stadiums around the country. Lifelong bonds were formed.

After the cleats were hung, the gloves tossed in the garage and the baseball awards collected dust, why did so many Orioles from this era choose to remain in the Baltimore area and fall in love with our city?

"We raised our children here and once the kids started in school, we got rooted," Ken said. "We made additional friends and didn't want to start all over again somewhere else. Baltimore is a place where people know us. Also, after our playing days, some business opportunities came along for some of us. Baltimore is a major city with a small town feel. It isn't six degrees of separation here, more like three – there is always somebody you know who knows someone else you know."

A good handful of Orioles from Ken's era continue to live in Baltimore: Brooks Robinson, Jim Palmer, Cal Ripken Jr., Billy Ripken, Scotty McGregor, Boog Powell, Tippy Martinez, Ross Grimsley, Al Bumbry, Joe Orsulak, Dick Hall, Dave Johnson, Bill Swaggerty, Ron Hansen and others. And before they died: Elrod Hendricks, Mark Belanger, Paul Blair and Mike Flanagan. These guys are (and were) Baltimoreans through and through. Most are still involved in the community and make appearances, and some still work in baseball. Truly, it's the Baltimore baseball bond.

Call a teammate; he'll come running

Utter the words *golf tournament* and former pro athletes will show up with their golf bags. Mention the phrase "kids with cancer" and generous teammates will come running in bunches.

The annual *Ken Singleton Celebrity Golf Classic* includes a handful of Ken's former teammates plus other sports and Hollywood celebrities golfing for this Cool Kids Campaign fundraiser. Cool Kids is a nonprofit organization based in Towson, Md., that assists kids with cancer, and their families. Ken serves on its board.

And when Ken's former teammates call him to participate in one of their charity golf tournaments, he grabs his clubs and goes. "When we were playing," Ken said, "we all had each other's backs. It's nice to know we still do."

This amazingly powerful organization (see story, Cool Kids Campaign established in Mark Belanger's honor) recognizes that these "cool kids" and their parents and siblings need distractions as they muddle through horrifically challenging months – sometimes years – of treatments, surgeries, hospitals, financial setbacks and parents watching their "babies" become bald and ill while enduring this vile disease.

"It was, of course, terrible to watch MacKenzie fight against the 'C-Monster,'" said Steve Stuck, father of the late MacKenzie Stuck, one of the original cool kids. "For years of appointments, surgeries, rehabilitation, radiation, chemotherapy, clinical trials, and experimental studies, as a parent, I felt ultimately helpless to save my child's life."

The impressive celebrity list at Ken's tournament has featured Hall of Famers Jim Palmer, Eddie Murray, Gary Carter and Brooks Robinson. Other former Orioles – Ken's friends – have committed their time as well: Tippy Martinez, the late Paul Blair, Boog Powell, Rick Dempsey, Bobby Floyd, Bobby Grich, Steve Rogers, Dick Hall and Joe Orsulak, among other retired players, TV hosts and entertainers. Other celebs on the links have included *Dancing With The Stars'* Tony Dovolani; NBA's Jack Marin; and NFL's Victor Green, Lydell Mitchell, Bruce Laird and Tom Matte.

The golfers leave the tournament with more than a silk-screened tote bag. They take with them images of young kids suffering through cancer. A few they meet at the pre-tournament banquet. Some of the kids, sadly, are no longer here, like MacKenzie Stuck, who rode around one of Ken's tournament at Hunt Valley Golf Club in 90-plus degree weather to greet the golfers in a festively decorated golf cart. The preteen's face was swollen from medication, yet her disposition was sweet. She had rounded third base with a brain tumor (it had returned three times) and after the fourth, when nothing more could be done, MacKenzie died.

During tournaments after that one, her parents were barely audible through their tears as they spoke to the golfers at the tournament dinner to stress the importance of Cool Kids Campaign's mission.

"Cancer changes a kid more than just physically; they have to grow up pretty fast in many ways," said Steve Stuck. "Through it all Kenz developed a tremendous compassion for others and selflessly did everything she could to make someone *else* feel better. In that regard, I sensed a similarity between my daughter, the Cool Kids staff, Ken and his family, and his baseball friends. It was very touching to see so many former star athletes and celebs – some of them heroes of my youth – in such a down-to-earth way; relating to cancer kids and their families on a human level and pitching in to make a difference with the most valuable resources we have – our time."

Yes, mention the words *golf tournament* and a group of jocks will show up. Yet it's for a much greater reason than chasing a miniature white ball around 18 holes. These guys call on each other in friendship, and in support of worthy causes. This time, it's for the kids.

When fans write to Ken requesting autographs, he signs the items and includes a note asking them to consider a donation to Cool Kids Campaign. As a result, the nonprofit organization has received thousands of dollars. To learn more about this organization, visit coolkidscampaign.org.

The late "cool kid" Nicolas Perez wearing a "Cancer Fears Me" chemo cap with NY Yankees manager ***Joe Girardi*** *in Yankee Stadium dugout. Nicolas was tutored in New York via Skype by a Cool Kids Campaign tutor in Baltimore.*

(next page top) ***Eddie Murray*** *and* ***Al Bumbry*** *play annually in the Ken Singleton Celebrity Golf Classic benefitting Cool Kids Campaign.*

(next page bottom) Golfers ***Bill Swaggerty, Ken Singleton, Eddie Murray, Joe Orsulak*** *and* ***Steve Rogers*** *at a tournament party.*

(Photos courtesy Cool Kids Campaign)

***Chris Federico**, Cool Kids Campaign president, and dancer **Tony Dovolani** of Dancing With the Stars fame, a previous golf tournament participant. (below) **Ken Singleton** hosts the annual Ken Singleton Celebrity Golf Classic fundraiser for Cool Kids Campaign, and serves on its board. (Photos courtesy Cool Kids Campaign)*

One name: Willie Mays

The Yankees had just departed San Francisco and Ken landed in Boston on a red eye, leaving behind the home of the Giants, where his all-time favorite baseball player, Willie Mays, played most of his career.

"He was a great all-around player," said Ken of the center fielder. "He was exciting, he made the right plays at the right time, was a great home run hitter, a tremendous fielder, and a great base stealer and base runner."

In Cooperstown 2007, when we attended Cal Ripken Jr.'s and Tony Gwynn's inductions into the Hall of Fame, Ken and I bumped into Willie Mays several times during the hectic weekend. The two had played against each other when Ken first arrived in the big leagues as a New York Met in 1970. In the first expansion of baseball to the West Coast, the Giants moved to San Francisco in the late 1950s, as did the Dodgers. That broke the heart of Ken's dad, Joe – he eventually got over it and began to root for the Mets.

Decades later, the face-to-face interaction with Mays clearly thrilled Ken. "If I had a ball, I would have asked him to sign it," he said, admittedly a bit nervous at the time. "I asked to take a picture together but I didn't want to be all over the guy, knowing how that feels."

Mays said he remembered Ken as a player, and asked if he was still announcing on TV. "Which I thought was nice," Ken said. "When I was a youngster, he was the man. He couldn't do anything wrong. I remember when the Giants moved."

Yet as a fan back then, he said, it was hard to follow the Dodgers and Giants. Communication wasn't nearly as effective as today.

"There was no DirectTV to watch every game," said Ken. "People back east wouldn't find out game results until the late edition of the newspaper came out. There's no telling how popular Willie Mays would have been if modern social media would have been available. He would have been even a bigger star."

Where-oh-where is that Richard Gere?

The wonderful husband and wife team Anthony and Adriana Taffuri, proprietors of A&A Car Service in New York City (which Ken uses through YES Network), once told me they sometimes drive Richard Gere. Cool.

Isn't he a grand actor, that Richard Gere? *Officer and a Gentleman, Pretty Woman, Nights in Rodanthe, Unfaithful, The Hoax* ... those are a few favorite Gere movies, although he thrives in all of them, if you ask this fan.

In Cooperstown 2007, when our family drove up for Cal Ripken Jr.'s Hall of Fame induction, I tried not to get too tickled knowing Gere was "in the building" during a VIP reception we attended in the Hall of Fame Museum. Yet in spite of trying to stay cool about spotting him, my "Hollywood antennae" rose as I nosed around the room, bypassing many famed ballplayers' faces, most of whom I've met repeatedly over the years, in hopes of zeroing in on one good actor.

Now where-oh-where is that Richard Gere? I couldn't find him anywhere. Darn. Maybe it was a rumor.

Then Ken and I strolled into the museum's art gallery. We stopped in front of a colorful Willie Mays oil painting (the "Say Hey Kid" is Ken's all-time favorite player; see story, One Name: Willie Mays) to snap a pic of Ken next to it. No one else was in the room. A few minutes later, in walked Gere and his young son. He spotted Ken and extended a handshake, introduced himself and relayed how he has enjoyed Ken's work on YES Network.

Wasn't that friendly? Here was a famous Hollywood movie star who constantly has fans gushing over him, praising my husband as a fan. I felt so proud of Ken!

If my tongue wasn't so twisted, I may have said something clever. (I don't actually remember what I blabbered.) The three of us posed together for a few photos; he introduced his son and we merrily moved along. We never spotted Gere again over the weekend, although he had to have attended the induction ceremony.

In the following day's newspaper, I noticed a front-page photo of John Travolta and his wife Kelly Preston seated in the front row at the Induction ceremony. Was I slipping? I hadn't spotted them at the ceremony, dang! That would have tickled me, too, as a longtime Travolta fan. I really need to get that antennae fixed.

*Suzanne & Ken with **Willie Mays** in Cooperstown, N.Y. 2007 Mays was Ken's baseball idol growing up. (below) Suzanne & Ken with actor **Richard Gere** in the Hall of Fame Museum's art gallery. (Singleton photos)*

When Carter was just a "Kid"

Death had been reaching out its long pasty fingers too often in 2012 in the baseball world. Fans and friends were saying farewell to a legend too young to die ... Gary Carter, 57, who died from brain tumors.

I mostly remember Gary and his wife, Sandy, from our days in Montreal in the 1990s, when Gary was a player and Ken was an Expos radio and TV broadcaster (1985-96). Extremely nice people those Carters, offering continuing smiles and kind words in the tunnel under Olympic Stadium after the games; and in the stands nearby as we wives and our kids watched games in the family section.

We have bumped into the Carters sporadically over the years in the baseball world; one of the more exciting places was in Cooperstown, N.Y., when Gary was inducted into the Hall of Fame along with Eddie Murray in 2003.

"He was a fan favorite," Ken said after Gary's death, in a radio interview from home on a station in Toronto, Canada; a Sports Center story about Gary aired low-volume on the television in the background. "His personality was infectious. He was the same way every day."

Ken and Gary were brief teammates in 1974 – for a month to be exact – as Gary the rookie was called up in September from the minor leagues while Ken played out his last month as an Expo; Ken was traded to Baltimore that winter. Gary was nicknamed "Kid" for his youthful exuberance.

"You could see the promise in him as a player," Ken said, "even for the short time when we were on the same team. Gary played probably the toughest position on the field and he did it well for a long time. It is rightly so that he's in the Hall of Fame."

Over the years Ken and Gary played against each other during spring training games and a few All-Star Games (there was no inter-league play then) and it was back in Canada where they met up once again – Ken in a different role. He had entered his second career as a baseball broadcaster, doing play-by-play on the radio in Montreal and color analysis on TV for The Sports Network (TSN).

"We were around each other every day," Ken said. "When Gary came back to Montreal he was already a star. He was on the back end of what would become his Hall of Fame career. Since I had seen him at his beginning, now I was watching him at the end of his career, too. He still played with the same rookie enthusiasm."

In the baseball world, as in life, people weave in and out of our lives. Gary and Ken were acquainted once again in 2009 when he invited Gary to participate in the *Ken Singleton Celebrity Golf Classic* in Baltimore – a major fundraiser for the Cool Kids Campaign for which Ken serves on its board.

"I was appreciative of his playing in the tournament," said Ken. "I had called him; he agreed to play. We were very fortunate to have had Gary come up from Florida to participate. It was a wonderful gesture – that's the way he was."

Gary Carter *autographs a baseball during the Ken Singleton Celebrity Golf Classic in Baltimore. Carter was inducted into the Hall of Fame in 2003. He died in 2012. (Photo courtesy Cool Kids Campaign)*

Baltimore is Tippy's sweet spot

It was like having another wife, said retired relief pitcher Felix "Tippy" Martinez, about the camaraderie he shared with fellow Orioles in the 1970s and -'80s. In their baseball marriage, they were more than teammates who wore black and orange on 33rd Street. They were a chummy group interlaced in life as neighbors, friends and godparents to each other's children.

"We seemed to get along really well," said 66-year-old Martinez, referring to former Orioles such as Rick Dempsey, Kiko Garcia, Len Sakata, Mark Belanger, Scott McGregor, Ken Singleton and others. "We signed five-year contracts so we were together longer. I'm still friends with them – that's the beauty of it." Tippy was a relief pitcher for the O's from 1976 to 1987. (Lifetime W-L record 55-42 with 3.45 ERA.)

As a team unto themselves outside the ballpark, their families socialized, vacationed at Deep Creek Lake and at the beach, and spent All Star breaks together. Whether hanging at each other's homes or riding on the team bus, the players bonded, said Martinez, as Orioles and friends. "We still joke around and have fun with each other now."

Maintaining friendships isn't the only steady factor in Tippy's post-pitching days. As he has held tight to his ballplayer buddies, he has also clung to Baltimore – and not only for his love of crabs. "Although if I lived somewhere else, I'd have them shipped to me!" he said.

Baltimore-area residents since 1976, the major leaguer and his high school sweetheart and wife of 46 years, Carol, live in Towson. They opted to remain in Charm City after Martinez's retirement, since their two children were rooted here and held an equal fondness for the only hometown they knew. Chasing after seven grandchildren now makes it unlikely the couple will ever return to Colorado to rejoin their families. (Tippy's hometown is LaJunta.)

What about Baltimore does Martinez like? "The people are nice," said the southpaw. "They treat their athletes with a lot of respect. Our fans grew up with us."

For almost six years, the Martinez couple bounced between Colorado and Maryland but eventually bought a one-way ticket. "I felt more accomplished training here in the off-season," said Martinez, "and my friends were here to train with."

It's never off-season now that he's out of the bullpen. Martinez is available to Baltimore fans through appearances at Orioles FanFest, Fantasy Camp and other O's celebrations. Autograph seekers can also find him at area golf courses swinging for Baltimore charities, including the *Ken Singleton Celebrity Golf Classic*.

"It's hard to say no to the charity events," said Martinez. "The outings are like reunions – I see many former teammates. It's nice to remain popular as an Oriole."

Tippy and Singy golf together as well on their own. They also socialize and vacation together, along with Byrd and Ross Grimsley, who pitched for the Orioles. Most notably, the couples appear on the annual baseball cruise operated by The Cruise Lady, on which a few dozen members of Oriole Advocates attend. Yet another Orioles pitcher, Dennis Martinez, hosts the Singys, Martinezes, McGregors (Scott), Al Bumbry and Eddie Murray in Nicaragua in his annual charity golf tournament; Dennis is a native of Granada, Nicaragua.

Tippy's cleats and glove are pushed to the back of the closet – prideful symbols of pitching for the Orioles. A little change-up in Martinez's pride now shows through his friends and the town of Baltimore – his sweet spot.

Tippy & Carol Martinez *and their two children in Memorial Stadium 1982; on right is* ***Ken*** *and his two older boys.* ***Gary Roenicke*** *#35 stands in background. (Singleton photo)*

*Lifelong friends **Ken Singleton, Tippy Martinez** and **Ross Grimsley** in 2013 during the annual Baltimore Baseball Cruise organized by The Cruise Lady Inc. The cruise was once planned by the late **Elrod Hendricks** and has continued for several decades. (Singleton photo)*

The Singys go to Cooperstown

A rumor circulated around Cooperstown, N.Y., that John Travolta strolled the streets with wife Kelly Preston during Cal Ripken Jr.'s Induction Weekend 2007 and no one noticed the Hollywood couple. True or not, who knows? (Personally, I would have noticed John Travolta if I had passed him!)

But let a former Baltimore Oriole walk down Main Street in the midst of the mayhem and excitement – with the greatest baseball players in history around town – and fans sniffed him out in seconds.

"Mr. Singleton! Can we take your picture?"
"Would you sign this baseball?"
"Hey Kenny! I'm a big fan!"

People do not flock to Cooperstown on induction weekends to see Hollywood. Not Travolta, not Richard Gere (whom we met; see story, Where-oh-where is Richard Gere?) or any other whispered celebrities' names rumored to attend the Hall of Fame festivities during the muggy weekend in a lakeside town. No, fans showed up to envelop baseball.

The slew of admirers dressed in orange and black cared more about scoring a player's autograph than sighting a movie star. They thrust out balls, bats, shirts and posters, counting themselves lucky that one Kenny Singleton happened to be walking through the thick crowd with his wife and kids, a souvenir T-shirt bag in hand.

The kiddies and I always feel proud when baseball fans spot my husband's face out of a crowd to convey their admiration 32 years after he set down his right-fielder's glove.

Our then 15-year-old son tried to count the number of times Ken shook a hand, posed for a picture, signed an autograph, waved to a fan or returned a greeting. He lost count.

Who knows if John Travolta signed any autographs while visiting Cooperstown? Maybe someone finally noticed him. Or maybe he would have had better luck dressed in an Orioles jersey.

Later, we entered the Baltimore Orioles private lawn party on Otsego Lake. I carried a digital camera in my purse, in spite of the invitation's verbiage: *No photographs and no autographs.* (What can I say? I broke a rule. It was an exceptional photo opp.)

I suppose event organizers in the Orioles' office figured we baseball families have seen enough of the sport's greatest moments not to care about capturing them in pictures. I had wanted to pull out my camera sooner, yet it remained dormant in my handbag, in spite of the itch to do so.

Then Cal Jr. walked in. Listen; if you're at a private party with Cal on the day before he is to be inducted into the National Baseball Hall of Fame, you *must* take his picture, whether or not you've greeted him countless times since marrying Mr. Singy. It's a sports milestone!

Then Eddie Murray walked in. And I *knew* I would have to take a picture of Eddie, whether or not he's our friend – or because he is. *C'mon, it's Eddie!-Eddie!-Eddie!*

Then when Cal, Eddie and Ken stood together talking baseball, I could wait no longer. I quickly unzipped my purse and whipped out the digital to click Ken posing with Eddie and Cal; Eddie posing with Ken and our kids; Cal shaking our daughter's hand; and Ken with his arm slung over Mike Flanagan's shoulder. (See *Inside the Singletons' Photo Album*)

It was a quick two-hour party and time to leave. But wait, Hubs, there's Earl Weaver! And look, over there is … !

***Ken** stops to sign an autograph for a fan along Main Street in Cooperstown, N.Y., during Hall of Fame Induction Weekend honoring **Cal Ripken Jr.** and **Tony Gwynn**. (Singleton photo)*

Ride of a lifetime through Cooperstown

The town's red open-air trolleys motored visitors up and down the streets of Cooperstown, N.Y., throughout Induction Weekend 2007 to honor Cal Ripken Jr. and Tony Gwynn. On the eve of the ceremony, those same trolleys transported Hall of Famers and former players to the National Baseball Hall of Fame for a private red-carpet reception.

Ken and I rode on one, thrilled to sit several seats behind Willie Mays and Harmon Killebrew, both Hall of Famers. Mays was Ken's favorite player growing up. (See story: One Name: Willie Mays).

As the vehicle exited the Otsego Hotel's gates, flashbulbs immediately lit up the summer night as hundreds of people lined the street in parade-like fashion. Video cameras scanned right to left as we passed. Orioles and Padres T-shirts covered torsos everywhere. Fans' necks stretched to glimpse the pros that were riding in our trolley. Though the darkness mostly hid the two baseball legends, the crowd cheered in general, knowing a baseball "somebody" was on the vehicle.

The closer we inched to 25 Main Street, the more boisterous the cheers, and the number of faces grew from hundreds to thousands. It was dream-like, surreal, thrilling and thoroughly exhilarating. It was the ride of a lifetime.

The last time I experienced such a baseball-related "rush" was during Cal Ripken Jr.'s 2,131 game at Oriole Park at Camden Yards in 1995. Over 45,000 fans screamed and chanted for No. 29 as Ken was introduced onto the field and I was escorted to the Orioles dugout to watch Cal accept the attention. Having stepped onto baseball fields hundreds of times to applause, Ken may be accustomed to that kind of head-spinning excitement, but I am not.

So there we were 12 years later, dressed to the nines, preparing to enter the Hall of Fame. After Mays and Killebrew stepped off the trolley and were introduced outdoors by the emcee, the rest of us walked a red carpet with dozens of TV cameras rolling and photographers shooting; and we entered the glass front doors.

Inside we spent the evening in the "shrine" of the museum among many Hall of Famers, a sprinkling of movie stars and long walls of bronze plaques symbolizing each inductee.

Of any Hall of Famer for Ken to have had the pleasure of following into the museum, Willie Mays tops the list – his all-time favorite player. In Mays' company, Ken was in his baseball glory.

"On a baseball field," Ken said, "Mays could do anything. When I see him, it takes me back to my childhood."

It's rare I'm able to witness my husband as an admiring fan. Usually the table is turned. Yet on this special evening, Ken was transfixed to baseball's past in a different era. As he said to our kids the next day, "It meant a lot to Dad to see those guys."

His pride and love of the game burst through as he introduced me one by one to the greats: Reggie Jackson, Wade Boggs, Carlton Fisk, Frank Robinson, Lou Brock, Joe Morgan, Rod Carew, and the late Yogi Berra and Tony Gwynn, the newest inductee. We hobnobbed with a parade of other pros, some of whom I had met previously. Ken considers himself blessed to have played with, and against, many of those talented men.

A party bonus presented itself when actor Richard Gere introduced himself to Ken, commenting on how he enjoys watching him broadcast the NY Yankees YES Network games. (See story, Where-oh-where is that Richard Gere?)

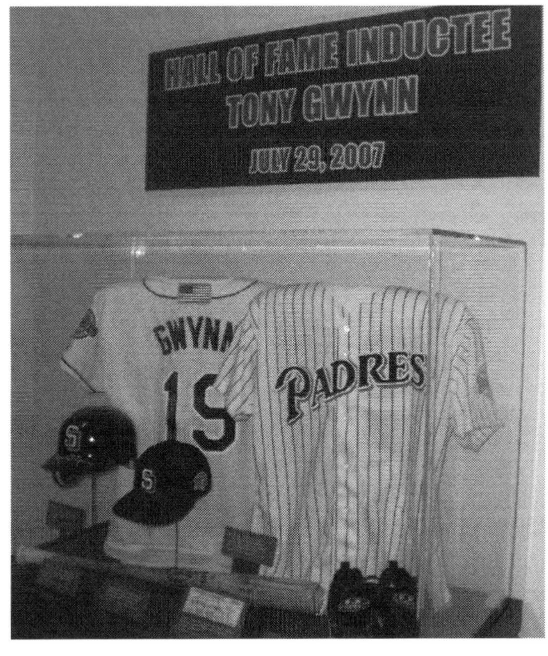

The reception was an adrenaline-pumping event – quite thrilling. It has been exciting over the years to be a small part of the making of baseball history where Cal was concerned: attending his 2,130 record-tying game, his 2,131 record-breaker and watching No. 8 take his final bow in an Oriole uniform in 2001.

We felt blessed to add Cooperstown to the list, having been there one other time for Eddie Murray's 2003 induction weekend. Ken has the added honor of saying he was Cal's teammate for three seasons, when the rookie first buttoned up a Baltimore Orioles jersey.

For this Cal fan – and every other – indeed it has been the ***gr8test*** ride of a lifetime.

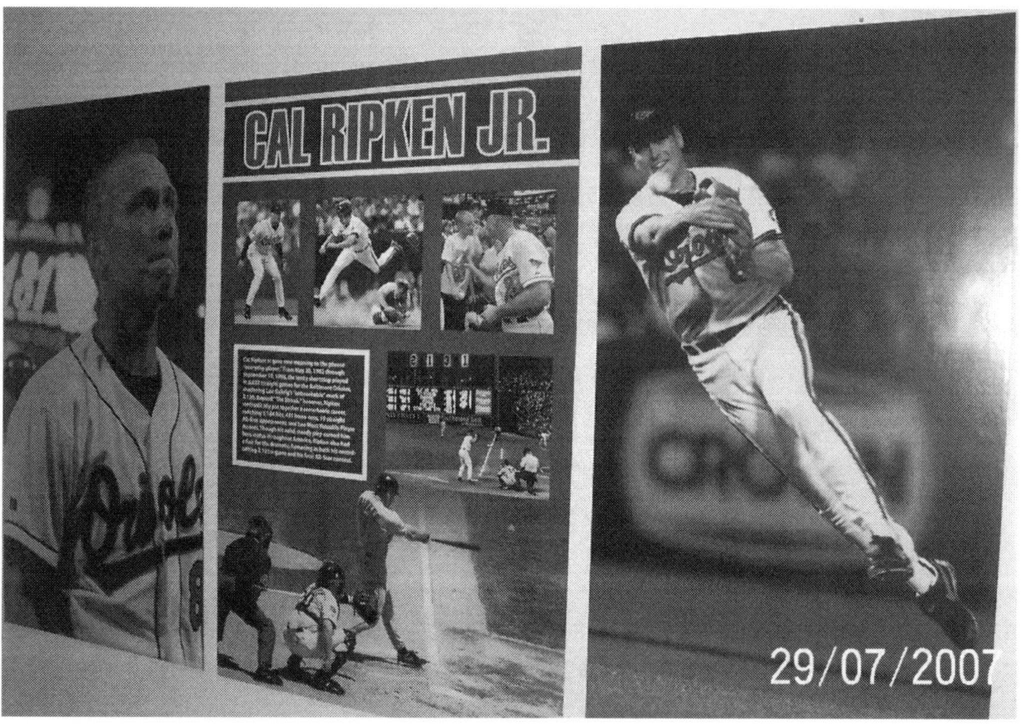

(previous page and above) Baseball Hall of Fame displays in Cooperstown, N.Y. on Induction Weekend 2007 of ***Cal Ripken Jr*** *and* ***Tony Gwynn****. (Singleton photos)*

Playing ball as an African-American in the 1960s

While watching the Jackie Robinson Day ceremony at Yankee Stadium one April, our friend Joe Ferraro from Smithtown, N.Y., commented about the current players: “These guys have no idea what black players went through back then." The Rangers and Yankees players each donned the number 42 for that particular game, as did all MLB players, in commemoration of the man who changed baseball.

Joe's comment inspired me to ask Ken on the ride back to the hotel after the game: What was it like as an African-American to play baseball in the 1960s?

"I'm not comparing what I experienced to what African-Americans and Hispanic players went through before me,” Ken said, “because they did all the heavy lifting. But it wasn't great sometimes. It was obvious in some of these cities that people weren't happy that black and Latino players were there – in the manner of speaking or the way people looked at us. They weren't nice. It didn't happen everywhere, but it did in certain places."

Ken played in the New York Mets' minor league system 1967-70 before being called up to the big leagues and never looking back: Winter Haven Florida (A); Raleigh Durham North Carolina (A); Vasalia California (A); Memphis Tennessee (AA) and Jacksonville Florida (AAA).

Although he was never the only black player on a team 20 years after Robinson paved the color warpath (called up in 1947), Ken was one of just a few. Growing up in integrated New York City schools prepared him to "learn how to get along with everyone," he said, as a student of Graham Junior High School and Mount Vernon High School. "I had all different nationalities of friends: Italian, Jewish, Black, Hispanic."

As a Montreal Expo, Ken had the good fortune once to meet Jackie Robinson in Jarry Park in Montreal (where the Brooklyn Dodgers had first sent Robinson to Triple A).

"I was taking batting practice and he came onto the field," Ken said. "I was tongue-tied. This guy was a legend! I was so nervous I was shaking. This was Jackie Robinson!"

As a right fielder, Ken recalls many a mean taunt from opposing fans jeering from the stands. "Fans yell stuff about your parents or your playing ability," he said, "They call out, 'You stink! You suck!' Not everyone at the ballpark was rooting for us."

Those incidents were mild compared to what Jackie Robinson experienced as the only black player in the entire league. "I don't know how he was able to do it," Ken said.

Pitchers threw at Robinson, opponents tried to spike him, fans insulted him, and Robinson received death threats that he would be killed if he showed up at a ballpark. Sadly, he was unable to lodge at the same hotel as his teammates. Robinson took all the heavy barbs for black players of the future.

"He had to hold his tongue – he must have been a very strong man," Ken said. "He was told he couldn't fight back – that he would have to take it. He was aware of the situation and where his success could lead to, not only personally, but also for all black players. Jackie Robinson was a social experiment for the whole country, and it paid off in baseball. If Robinson had failed, it would have set the country back many years. Who knows how long it would have taken to give another black player a chance?"

All of baseball owes this guy a debt of gratitude since baseball today is international, housing Hispanics, Europeans, Asians, Americans, to name a few, and certainly, scores of African-Americans.

Ken is convinced, as are many others in baseball, that "Robinson made the game better."

"Yo! Mrs. Singy!" calls Al Bumbry

An energetic and lively "Yo! Mrs. Singy!" is how Al Bumbry greets me on the phone when he calls the house.

We call him simply *Bee.* Ken also calls him "Little Boomer" – and a friend for life. Bee is a former teammate who once wore No. 1 on his white, orange and black Baltimore Orioles jersey.

We once lived in the same Baltimore County neighborhood as Bee until we moved 20 minutes north to the country in 1996. Bee had often walked down the street to visit us, with his then young son Steven who later enjoyed a career in the Orioles minor leagues.

Bee was a great neighbor – extremely helpful and always looking out for our family when Ken was on the road nonstop from March to September during his radio and television announcing days for the Montreal Expos.

Al even raked and gathered the plethora of leaves on our wooded property. He cut our grass and dabbled in a bit of creative landscaping, seemingly enjoying the yard work. He had offered to fix, haul and assist in anything a neighbor would do for another neighbor. We've given each other rides to the airport, and he brings us garden gifts: bell jars filled with his delicious homemade applesauce, or sacks of apples and peaches.

On several occasions when Ken was at work in Canada, Al played superhero when our wayward house alarm decided to announce itself in the middle of the night, scaring me to near-death as I snatched up the phone to call Bee. I was convinced the bogeyman was lurking nearby.

His "Yo, Mrs. Singy" wasn't as energetic and lively at 3 a.m. but his friendship remained true to form. In less than five minutes, Al showed up in sweats at the front door and walked around the perimeter of the house to make sure the bogeyman lurked only in my imagination. Once he even slept on the couch in the living room after the police had responded to a false alarm, so I would feel better protected home alone with young kids. Ballplayers are so brave.

Al is one of the smiliest people I have ever met. Great attitude, happy-go-lucky, and always offering wise words.

"Bee was a fantastic teammate and is an even better friend," said Ken about his best friend.

Al … the Bee … Little Boomer … who had coached our son Justin's York Revolution baseball team in York, Pa. … who has stood alongside Ken and other former Orioles as they supported their former team at special Camden Yard stadium events … whom we've spent time with in St. Croix and Nicaragua during charity golf tournament fundraisers for kids … who took up golf later in life so he and Singy could compete against each other … who visits our home to sit elbow-to-elbow with his long-time buddy to watch a boxing match, Super Bowl, NCAA Final Four, a baseball game or whatever other sport is trending.

Yo! Bee! Thanks for the friendship … and for my nickname.

*Former Oriole **Al Bumbry** and the Singletons remain close friends. Pictured is Mrs. Singy and "Bee" at the Orioles 60th anniversary celebration at Camden Yards 2014. (Singleton photo)*

Nutty nicknames add to baseball lore

Are nicknames named after "Nick," another name for Nicholas? Who knows, but nicknames can be amusing – and meaningful. Ken's "Singy" nickname was bestowed on him decades ago by Orioles teammates. It was then passed onto one of his three sons, Justin "Singy" Singleton, when he played baseball at Clemson University and up through Triple A.

Nicknames always have been common in the sports world. The 1900s featured "Wee Willie" Keeler, such nicknamed because he was small, and further back to the late 1800s, there was a Major Leaguer nicknamed "Death to Flying Things" – Bob Ferguson's nickname derived from his greatness as a defensive player.

Maybe the most famous nickname of all was "The Babe" for George Herman Ruth. No more needs to be said about him.

"We all had nicknames," Ken said. "But nicknames nowadays are more a derivative of the player's name instead of their talent."

Tippy Martinez's birth name is Felix, but he had the nickname 'Tippy' already before he entered baseball. There was "Cakes" for Jim Palmer because he ate pancakes on the days that he pitched since pitchers tend to be superstitious; "Blade" for the late Mark Belanger because he was so slim; and "El Presidente" for pitcher Dennis Martinez, the first player in the big leagues to hail from Nicaragua. "I gave him that nickname," Ken said, "and it stuck."

Tony Chavez was nicknamed "Visa Presidente" as in vice president. The team used to tease Tony and Dennis by asking, "Who's watching the country while you guys are away?" (Incidentally, Tippy and Dennis are not related.)

There was "Little Boomer" for teammate Al Bumbry (see previous story), nicknamed after Boomer Scott of the Boston Red Sox because both wore similar puka shell necklaces, in style at the time. He is also known as "Bee" since Bumbry simulates the word bumblebee.

Here are a few interesting nicknames around the league that Ken remembers as a kid rooting for the Giants; his dad Joe Singleton was a Dodgers fan.

- Willie “Puddinhead” Jones (Phillies’ third baseman in the 1950s)
- Eldon John “Rip” Repulski (Phillies outfielder); Cal Ripken Jr. also was called “Rip”
- George “Foghorn” Myatt (Phillies third base coach) “He had a very deep voice,” Ken said, “like the cartoon character Foghorn Leghorn.”
- Andre Dawson was nicknamed “The Hawk” - he ran down everything
- “The Cobra” had a quick strike in Dave Parker
- Terry Crowley was “The King of Swing” as a good pinch hitter
- “Pops” was Willie Stargell since he was older than some players

There was “Rocket” (Roger Clemens) and “Dominican Dandy” (Juan Marichal, a Hall of Fame pitcher for the Giants) whom Ken liked growing up and “got to play against later. I hit two home runs off of him,” he said.

“The Bird” was a Detroit Tigers pitcher, the late Mark Fidrych, since he resembled the Sesame Street character *Big Bird*. He used to talk to the ball to tell it what to do; he also went down on his hands and knees to groom the dirt on the mound.

“The Wizard” was Ozzie Smith “because he was a great fielder,” Ken said, and “The Kid” was Gary Carter because “he was enthusiastic as a kid.” (see story, When Carter was just a “Kid”).

Around the Yankees clubhouse mid-2000, Derek Jeter was known as “Jetes” or “The Captain,” as in captain of the team. Nick Swisher was “Swish;” Mariano Rivera was “Mo;” and Curtis Granderson was “Grandy.” Freddy Garcia was called “The Chief” since he resembles the character of the same name in the movie “One Flew Over the Cuckoo’s Nest.”

There are players who have built-in nicknames, such as “A.J.” for Allan James Burnett and “CC” for Carsten Charles Sabathia, both former Yankees. In the broadcast booth was Jim “Kitty” Kaat, Ken’s former Yankees broadcaster. (See story, Meeting Mrs. Kitty Kaat.)

Still with the Yanks is Alex Rodriquez, first to be called “A-Rod” by the late Dave Neihaus, Seattles Mariner broadcaster, when Alex began his career with the Mariners. Mark Teixeira is “Tex,” following his father John’s nickname.

“Nicknames are like terms of endearment,” Ken said, “they’re less formal. It shows that you appreciate the player – the teammate – and are willing to give him a name.”

Happy Birthday Cal Ripken Jr. & Papa Louie!

After I had posted a story on the *Mrs. Singy: Married to Baseball* column about a Yankees fan's dad's birthday, I had a case of Catholic guilt and decided I had better wish *my* father a happy 80th. Papa Louie shares his Aug. 24 birthday with Cal Ripken Jr. – I'm sure Cal has it noted on his calendar.

When Cal turned 30, Ken and I were invited to the nearby Ripken estate for a pool party. A Calypso band played, a scrumptious buffet was available and plenty of baseball celebs milled around. A fun night.

I remember trying to walk inside the house to use the ladies' room and a lone guy stood near the back door.

"Hi," I said. "Are you waiting to use the bathroom?" ... "No," he replied. "I'm the security guard." ... Oh, oops.

Back in 1959, there was no Calypso band, gourmet buffet or security guard for Papa Louie's 30th birthday. Just baby number three (me) popping out a month-and-a-half later screaming her head off. I haven't shut up yet.

My dad was a real card before dementia took over – a silly and funny guy. Typical loud Italian bricklayer. A splendid father. Proud of his kids. Sang goofy songs to the grandchildren. Totally illogical (we call it "Louie Logic.") Fixed everything in our houses the "Louie way." Introduced my mom Gina as his "first wife." He cracked up the entire family. He is "Uncle Louie" to many and everyone adores him. And he was a baseball fan.

Just ask Kenny about the father-in-law he adored. Whisper "Louie" to him and he'll laugh, I promise. Louie was the guy with the lampshade on his head at a party – literally. Good thing we didn't take him to Cal's 30th birthday party.

*Ken's father-in-law, **Louie Molino**, 87, shares the same birthday with **Cal Ripken Jr.** Louie died August 22, 2016. (Singleton photos)*

"… people will come, Ray. They'll come to Iowa for reasons they can't even fathom …They'll arrive at your door as innocent as children, longing for the past … And they'll walk out to the bleachers; sit in shirtsleeves on a perfect afternoon. They'll find they have reserved seats somewhere along one of the baselines, where they sat when they were children and cheered their heroes. And they'll watch the game and it'll be as if they dipped themselves in magic waters.

The memories will be so thick they'll have to brush them away from their faces … The one constant through all the years, Ray, has been baseball. America has rolled by like an army of steamrollers. It has been erased like a blackboard, rebuilt and erased again. But baseball has marked the time. This field, this game: it's a part of our past, Ray. It reminds us of all that once was good and it could be again. Ohhhhh, people will come Ray. People will most definitely come."

~ narrative from the film Field of Dreams, 1989

2nd INNING

The Fanatic Fans

(and some bizarre items in Ken's fan mail)

That lady wins for "Most Excited Fan"

There are three things my husband dislikes: cursing, drunk women and fans that go over the top when noticing him in public.

She wasn't drunk and she didn't swear, but a female sales rep in a furniture store once became super excited when Ken Singleton walked in. We were there to purchase an easy chair for his dad Pop Singy, yet gauging by this woman's reaction, you would have thought we were hosting a Baltimore Orioles team parade past her desk.

Recognizing Ken immediately launched her fully into what I call "fanatic fan" mode ... someone who becomes extremely nervous and excited because s/he has spotted Ken and reacts a tad over-the-top. In case you haven't witnessed that scenario, it goes something like this, exhaled all in one breath:

"OH MY GOSH!!! It's Ken Singleton!!!
You're Ken Singleton, right??!! The ball player??
You are, aren't you?? You used to play for the Orioles??
I can't believe Ken Singleton just walked in!!
Oh my gosh!! I need to get an autograph!!

Can I have your autograph??
I should take your picture!! Can I take your picture??
Wait, do I even have a camera?? Or a pen?? Do you have a pen??
Oh my gosh, I have to call my husband,
he's never going to believe this!!"

And with continued exclamation points, the woman ran to her desk to call her spouse to announce the big news.

We escaped between the rows of furniture, selected a comfy-looking, rose-colored easy chair for Pop, and vamoosed out of the store before Fanatic Fan could tackle Ken and tie him to a piece of furniture.

I've witnessed other fans react "happily" when they spotted my husband out and about doing ordinary human things (being that he's an ordinary guy who buys milk and dog food), but this lady wins for Most Excited Fan, using the shrillest voice to have ever reverberated throughout Baltimore.

A boy can dream

Then 9-year-old Nicholas Ziff with a nifty crew cut announced confidently to Ken at a Bernie Williams' performance in Longboat Key, Fla., a few years back, "One day I'm going to play first base for the New York Yankees." Williams was the guitar-playing 16-year center fielder for the New York Yankees, now retired as a player and enjoying a second career as a Latin jazz musician.

Nicholas Ziff of Sarasota, Florida told Ken that one day he wants to play for the New York Yankees. (Photo courtesy Ziff family)

"Keep practicing, Nick," encouraged Ken, kneeling next to him on the beach to snap a photo, as he has told other young boys who have voiced their dreams of playing professional baseball.

A dream – of any caliber – begins with a passion, an idea and certainly a declaration. When something invades your soul, seeps into your bones and plants itself in your mind permanently, there is no reason why it cannot materialize.

Little Nicholas may change his mind about playing baseball as he grows up – or not. Surely many a Major Leaguer had declared the same self-assured sentence during their Little League days. Williams had the passion to play baseball and music – and has done both beautifully. Derek Jeter wanted to play shortstop for the Yankees when he was a little boy, just like Nicholas – and we know the rest of that story. Ken realized his baseball future at age 5.

With enough diligence and hard work, dreams can transform into reality. Anything can begin with a strong affirmation. If Nick repeats that sentence enough times, and believes in his baseball talent and the ability to make it happen ... mark his words. Maybe one day we will see Nicholas Ziff, a Yankees fan from Sarasota, playing first base in Yankee Stadium.

It's all about holding the vision. Keep practicing, Nicholas – and keep affirming your dream.

Baseballs and bats magically appear when Singy is near

I do not know any magicians personally, but I have watched baseball fans magically pull out bats and baseballs from thin air when they stumble across Ken out in public – as if they are magicians themselves.

After an Orioles/Yankees game in Baltimore one night, a friend of a friend – Don, a devoted Orioles fan – was able to meet and greet Ken after the game on the way to our car. Don had conveniently whipped out a baseball and asked Ken to sign it. He did not have a pen, however. (Rookie mistake!) I lent Don a pen; a writer *always* has a pen.

Although not so surprising that Don happened to have a baseball with him, since he was attending a game, over the years I cannot name how many times this very scenario has played out in a non-baseball setting. It's quite amazing.

On one of my birthdays, Ken and I were dining out with four close friends in Baltimore's Little Italy, when a guy spotted Ken in the restaurant. The fan approached our table with a baseball bat and asked for an autograph.

I had to laugh. "You just happened to have a baseball bat with you?" I asked. He laughed in return and said, "I just got it for my birthday." We glanced over to his group of friends a few tables away who were clearly in celebration mode.

Another time while waiting for a movie to start at the Senator Theatre, Ken and I stopped for a beverage in a venue next door, where a fan spotted him. He walked over, introduced himself and whipped out two baseballs from his pockets. (Who goes to the movies with baseballs in their pockets?)

If fans don't have a tangible item to autograph, they make do with napkins, scraps of paper, menus, or whatever else nearby they can grab fast enough before the baseball celeb gets away. All part of the territory – and most interesting to watch.

However, sometimes fans do cross the line. One summer Friday night, before the Open Air Film Fest began (again in Little Italy), a fan had run down the street after us and wanted Ken to follow him back to a restaurant a block away, to meet his friends.

"We're kinda on a date here," I said to the guy, friendly enough, hopefully. (I just wanted time with my husband.)

Then sometimes while we're out in public, no one recognizes Ken at all … yet we're always waiting for it.

Here is the most unbelievable one, and this is the truth … a hospital staff employee asked Ken for an autograph at absolutely the *most inappropriate* moment – while I was in labor.

Oh boy! (And it *was* a boy.) If I could have pulled a bat out of thin air myself …

Coconut macaroons in Ken's fan mail?

With the oodles of boxes and envelopes – large and small, bulky and flat, neat and sloppy – that over the years have entered our house from autograph-seekers, I've sort of become immune to them. Fan mail is scattered everywhere in the house – on Ken's desk, in the easy chairs, on the dresser, and in the kitchen where the paper pile waits for the administrative assistant to process (don't be impressed – she and I are the same person).

Yet once in a while the contents of an envelope, spread across the kitchen table after Ken opens the mail, sparks my interest and I'll pick up a letter, look at a Ken Singleton baseball card, or marvel at a small plastic container of coconut macaroons. *Did I say coconut macaroons?*

In the category of "interesting things people mail to Ken," a longtime Yankees fan named Joyce Rockwood of New York City baked a batch of "Joyce's Yummy Homemade Macaroons." After first delivering them to Yankee Stadium where Ken works, the cookies were rejected there, so Joyce mailed her package with a nicely scrawled note that suggested Ken share the cookies in the YES Network booth.

Joyce had painstakingly placed a thoughtful selection of other items into the box along with her friendly letter: a coffee table Orioles book photographed by her dad; a photo of a younger Joyce in Bucky Dent's locker in 1978; a current photo of Joyce with a baseball glove on her head next to her husband at Yankee Stadium that the camera crew happened to post on TV; her business card; carefully hand-rolled coconut macaroons; and the recipe in case Ken felt like baking in the offseason. (Actually he bakes only chocolate cakes – see story, *Please no more chocolate cake!*)

I emailed Joyce to thank her for the entire package and said, "If we lived in a perfect world, baseball husbands would have time to respond to each piece of fan mail." Then I said, "If I liked coconut at all, I would have tasted what I'm certain must be the yummiest macaroons ever baked by a Yankees fan." (Coconut-wise, Malibu Coconut Rum is as far as I venture.)

People such as Joyce who take the time to do such fun gestures, and are determined that a package reach its destination, are surely to be applauded.

There are other fans out there who also should be thanked one by one. Where is that darn administrative assistant when you need her?

More fan mail: reindeer meat from Denmark

Move over, Joyce's Coconut Macaroons (previous story), the Singletons have received a new contender for the most unique item included in Ken's fan mail — three cans of reindeer and elk meat from Horsholm, Denmark.

Former New Yorker Larry Landman included a neatly typed letter pointing out that during the playoffs that last season, Ken had thanked fans on the East Coast for staying up late to watch the Yankees play on the West Coast, but had inadvertently omitted the fans outside of Copenhagen who were watching the next day via Internet.

"We did not stay up late, that's true," Larry wrote, "but we were rooting for the Yankees as strongly as anyone. We thank you and your fellow broadcasters on TV and radio for giving us a little taste of home while we live abroad. Given the beauty – the absolute beauty – of condensed [Internet] games, we have seen more Yankees games the last few years than while growing up and living in New York."

Ken was awed as he studied the letter and the three cans of meat sitting on the kitchen table. "I didn't know people in Europe were watching!"

We were all too curious to see what reindeer meat looked like, so our then 17-year-old son, Dante, bee-lined for the can opener. Yet who would be brave enough to taste it? Six-foot-three teenage boys eat anything, so no surprise that Dante volunteered. And since I had once tasted reindeer sausage on a cruise excursion through Alaska – and lived to tell about it – I fished two forks out of the utensil drawer.

"Is it cooked?" I asked, staring at the blob of raw-looking red meat peeking from under the jagged lid. We read the label, the majority of which was written in Danish except for the ingredients — and we had already used our imagination for that. We each stabbed a tiny forkful.

"It tastes like … um …," said Dante.

"Chicken?" I joked.

"No, I can't put my finger on it," he said, "but I'm not crazy about the aftertaste." Ken put no fingers, fork or tongue on any of it. "I'll give you 24 hours," he joked. "If nothing happens to you two, I'll taste it."

As a group of friends were scheduled to visit our home that Friday evening, Ken had a bit more fun with the topic: “Make an hors d’oeuvre out of it,” he suggested. “Think our friends would know?”

Dear Larry Landman: We apologize for the jokes, but please understand that reindeer meat is a new concept for the Singletons. We eat seafood in Baltimore, Maryland.

All joshing aside, we were touched by Larry’s gift and laminated letter, especially the last sentence, a request that Ken enjoy the delicacy during spring training with fellow broadcasters: “Open a bottle of red wine and say a toast in memory of Bobby Murcer, and particularly Phil Rizzuto, whose admonition that one should not try to hit a home run, just a single, applies far, far beyond baseball.”

A contender for the most unique item included in Ken’s daily fan mail – three cans of reindeer and elk meat from a Yankees fan in Denmark. (Singleton photo.)

From a Japanese friend, Fu-chan; Friends half a globe away share baseball passion

In Japanese, Ken knows how to say *happy birthday, thank you, good morning, good luck*, "and that's about it," he laughs. "I couldn't recite the Gettysburg Address or anything."

On Ken's first Major League trip to Japan in 1979 on an All-Star tour, he met Fumihiro "Fu-chan" Fujisawa, president of the Association of American Baseball Research.*

"He was very helpful," said Ken. "He could speak with us without a translator – his English was pretty good. He took us to his house, took us shopping, and made sure we didn't get lost on the extensive train system."

Ken and Fu-chan had the luck to meet again in 1984 when the then-World Champion Baltimore Orioles visited and played in Tokyo.

Through the years, Fu-chan and Ken have forged a long-distance friendship via mail and email, kept alive by their mutual love of baseball. Before each season, Fu-chan asks Ken for predictions of how American teams will finish in each division; who might be deemed an MVP; and who might win the Cy Young Award.

"Fu-chan has been a good friend over the years," Ken said, touched that this "very nice and gentle man" closes his emails with the words, "your friend."

On Ken's third trip to Japan in 2004, the black-haired petite Japanese man sat in the YES Network booth between him and Michael Kay during a telecast when the Yankees played a Japanese team. Off-air, Fu-chan relayed stories and information via handwritten notes and between-inning conversations, which only a Japanese baseball insider would know.

When the Yankees landed on American soil again, George Steinbrenner was waiting at the St. Petersburg airport to greet the team at 3 a.m. The owner called over Ken and Michael to compliment them.

"I didn't know you knew so much about Japanese baseball," Steinbrenner said, whereby Ken admitted their secret weapon had appeared in the form of a friend.

"The telecast would not have been the same without him," Ken said. "He knew the details to make the game interesting." (A detail such as knowing one of the player's names translated to "red star." Director John Moore was then able to show a close-up of that center fielder wearing a red glove.)

"Fu-chan knows Japanese and American baseball," Ken said. "Obviously he's a big fan." He has traveled to the United States to watch baseball around the country, and has met up with Ken in Baltimore and other cities, even staying overnight as a guest in the Singleton home.

As a Baltimore Oriole, Ken traveled to Japan twice with the team – in 1979 and 1984. On the first trip he befriended ***Fu-chan Fujisawa*** *(next page) and has since maintained contact. Pictured above is Ken in the dugout with a friend of Fu-Chan. In 2004, Ken again traveled to Japan with the New York Yankees as a TV analyst. (Singleton photos)*

In an email to Mrs. Singy, Fu-chan remembered the time in 2003 he had taken a photo of one of his sons with Hideki Matsui in Baltimore. Fu-chan had asked Ken to ask Hideki to sign it and mail it back.

"The picture flew to the USA over the Pacific Ocean," Fu-chan said, "and came back to Japan! I think it is a very good story of showing Ken's great personality and our friendship."

Back when Ken visited Japan as an Oriole, no Japanese players were in the Major Leagues. MLB had sent not only All-Star teams on tour, but the World Champions periodically had traveled to Tokyo on goodwill trips to play Japanese teams.

"Each time it was tougher to beat them," Ken remembered. "The Japanese were learning the game."

Today more Japanese players are in the states, like the former Yankee Hideki Matsui. Most teams in both U.S. leagues have added Japanese players to their rosters.

"It's a big deal when they get to come over here and play," Ken. Some American teams with Japanese players telecast their games to Japan live, for example, the Yankees, Seattle Mariners, and Boston Red Sox, which means fans a half globe away are watching today's game tomorrow (with the 13-hour time difference). "I bet fans DVR a lot of games."

When the late Hideki Irabu was a Yankee, Ken and I once met him and his translator George for lunch at Ken's favorite sushi restaurant, Edo Sushi, here in Baltimore County.

George was necessary because, remember, Ken only knows four Japanese phrases. (Besides English, I know only Italian, so I just ate my sushi.)

Using a translator is quite an interesting method in which to converse with another human being. That is the definition of trust! As avid sushi lovers, it was the first time Ken and I had eaten eel; Hideki had suggested it. Who were we to argue? The man knew his fish.

**The Association of American Baseball Research (AABR) was established in1977 in Tokyo, Japan. It releases, translates, and supervises books about American baseball, histories of teams, and MLB almanacs.*

Ken interviews Fu-chan for WJZ-TV 13 sports at the Singleton home during Fu-chan's visit to the U.S. with his family. After he retired from the field, Ken started his broadcasting career as a weekend sports anchor with Baltimore's WJZ. (Singleton photo)

Yankee Frankie: A 101-year-old fan

***Frankie Ventre**, an avid Yankee fan, lived to age 103. (Photo courtesy Annie Polk)*

Our neighbor Annie Polk had emailed me about a "most delightful" scene she witnessed while shopping in a grocery store in Hilton Head, S.C. An announcement was heard over the store's P.A. system: "Frank Ventre is 101 years old!" about one of its customers.

Annie said the store's staff had thoughtfully presented a few gifts representing Frank's interests in the way of blue and white goodies to delight him in his passion for the New York Yankees. While Frank received the gifts, he spoke about the team's championships, in what city they were playing that day, and where they would be playing. Frank knew his facts.

When he nostalgically mentioned how he wished he could again attend a game some day, but "the tickets are too expensive," Annie approached him.

Without mentioning the name of her neighbor Ken Singleton, she said she might be able to help him grant his wish. That's when she emailed to ask Ken if it was possible to obtain tickets for Frank. Ken arranged it, and Frank attended a game against the Tampa Bay Rays in New York.

As Ken double-checked the date, he chuckled, "How about that? It's Old-Timers' Day at Yankee Stadium."

When Ken had relayed the story to the Yankees Public Relations office, they sent Frank a letter inviting him onto the field before the game. A little old-timer recognition can go a long way. Frank's only disappointment was that Yogi Berra was scheduled to be in attendance, yet was admitted to the hospital a few days beforehand; Frank had looked forward to meeting the great legend.

"Oh my, I can't believe it!" Frank relayed to Annie, who told us, "He was so very excited! Ken should feel very pleased for having done that for him. What a life highlight for him!"

At age 101, Frank golfed weekly, and exercised at the gym five days a week. One hundred percent Italian, he was a sweet and entertaining man, Annie said. He was 103 when he died.

"Hats off to the grocery store staff – and the Yankees – that took time and effort merely to be nice," said Annie, "and to make an amazing old man feel very special."

The Cooperstown Gang

This friendly baseball-crazed bunch (in 2003) meets every July for Induction Weekend in Cooperstown, N.Y. at the Rose and Thistle Bed & Breakfast. The inn was established by New York Yankees fans, ***Patti D'Esposito****, and her late husband* ***Steve D'Esposito.*** *(Singleton photo)*

If you have not experienced the quaint village of Cooperstown in scenic upstate New York, please add it to your "must go" list. Cooperstown satiates visitors for its lovely location on Otsego Lake, its line of dazzling impeccable Victorian homes and its diverse collection of shops and restaurants, to name a few characteristics.

For baseball fans, add to the mix the National Baseball Hall of Fame and Museum on Main Street and surely Cooperstown bats a home run in perfect getaways.

Ken, the kids, and I have visited Cooperstown twice – in support of Ken's pals Eddie Murray and Cal Ripken Jr., former Oriole teammates inducted into the Hall of Fame in 2003 and 2007, respectively.

For a switch, we had opted to stay in a bed & breakfast versus a hotel. Online I had found a charming and well-kept Victorian house on Chestnut Street – The Rose and Thistle, less than a mile from the Main Street bustle.

Perfect choice. Two Yankees fans own it. Patti and (the now late) Steve D'Esposito from New Jersey had moved upstate in 2002 to try their hands at innkeeping, after working in Manhattan's rat race their entire careers. Let me assure you … this couple chose the perfect occupation.

We stayed for several nights at their inn and were hit with hospitality, warmth and graciousness unequaled at any hotel. Plus we met who we had labeled The Cooperstown Gang – a group of the most die-hard baseball fans I've ever encountered: Larry, Joan and Henry of N.J; Pat and Jim of N.Y.; Scott of Conn.; and Agatha, Steve and Steve Jr. of N.J. Most are Yankees' fans, with some Braves, Dodgers and Mets faithful in the mix, who meet year after year at The Rose and Thistle to celebrate baseball and the Hall of Fame's inductees.

This bunch of extremely friendly folks welcomed the newest family, the Singletons, to their annual gathering with open arms; of course, it didn't hurt that one of us happened to be a baseball announcer for the NY Yankees.

"They are baseball junkies who are pranksters, and lovable like family," said Patti of her Hall of Fame crew.

When Patti and Steve had announced to them that Ken Singleton would be staying at the inn, "Jim started to stutter and shake," Patti said, "and almost spilled his coffee. Henry was close to tears upon meeting Ken and said it was the best experience in his life. Larry was impressed with the amount of time Ken spent with our guests – he said he didn't want to wash his shoulder after Ken hugged him!"

Our welcome by this lovely group was astonishing – what a splendid weekend! Each morning, Steve slapped a scrumptious abundant breakfast on the large dining room table like your stomach wouldn't believe, and the D'Espositos treated their guests as family, even hosting a "porch barbeque" after the induction ceremony.

As we departed after our first visit, they promised to save us the top floor room for Cal Ripken Jr.'s induction in 2007. And do you know they did? We revisited Cooperstown, stayed at their wonderful B&B, and reacquainted with The Cooperstown Gang during an equally wonderful weekend, if not better.

"Everyone was humbled and honored to be in the Singleton family's company," Patti said.

Yet it was our family who felt humbled to be that welcomed, and to stay connected, to such a wonderful baseball bunch – the Cooperstown gang. Larry, Joan and Henry have visited Baltimore; and we have met up in other N.J. towns to say hello.

If I were writing a travel column, the Rose and Thistle would be awarded five stars. Visit their beautiful inn, *The Rose and Thistle*. Tell them the Singletons sent you.

Rosie: A little Italian lady talks Yankees

It's always amusing when a little old lady is a baseball fan – Ken gets a kick out of that, especially in light of his grandmother, Quinella Hathaway, who was a Chicago Cubs fan until she died at age 101.

Rosie Apicella, then 82, met Ken on the bocce courts in Baltimore's Little Italy, during my Tuesday night bocce league. Ken had tagged along to watch our team, *Cugini* (cousins), consisting of Molino cousins. However, he never had a chance to watch after Rosie found him.

And when Rosie found him, she talked baseball – lots of baseball. Mostly Yankees – she's a colossal Yankees fan. And that's surprising in a town that has its own baseball team, especially Baltimore fans true to their O's.

Rosie knew it was Derek Jeter's birthday and his age. She liked Robinson Cano; she knew Nick Swisher was starting to get hot. As Ken reported the current game score to Rosie from his phone, Swisher had just hit a home run.

"She knew more about the Yankees than I did!" Ken joked.

During Rosie's storytelling, she relayed one memory of a trip with her husband to New York to the old Yankee Stadium to see Joe DiMaggio play. "The Yankees lost," she said.

"When Joe played," Ken said, "there were no major league Orioles, so she had to root for someone. I don't blame her. He was a great player. Everyone liked him. Joe was the most popular baseball player and as you would expect, he had a huge Italian following."

One evening, Rosie had cooked dinner for Orioles pitcher Jeremy Guthrie when he lived in Little Italy. She met him as he pedaled past her house on a bike. "I was the only one who recognized him," she said. "He called me *Rosinda*."

Ken enjoyed his chat with Rosie. "She's a very enthusiastic and tremendous baseball fan," he said, "A very nice lady." She's also one of the better bocce players in Little Italy. She knows all about that sport, too – one she has been playing for most of her life. In bygone days, the Italian men wouldn't let girls play, but later Rosie helped to form the first all-female bocce team in Little Italy.

The dark clouds rolled in faster than we could roll bocce balls that night and it began to rain. Rosie flashed a crooked smile Ken's way and said as she dashed off to her rowhouse a few blocks over, "I'm gonna go finish watching the Yankee game."

*On Baltimore's Little Italy bocce courts, neighborhood resident **Rosie Apicella** talks Yankees with Ken. (Singleton photo)*

When it's Ken they really want

People are funny without realizing it – and a little transparent. If you were married to a doctor, would you be expected to answer medical questions? If you lived with a singer, would people expect you to break out in song?

So why do people expect me to talk baseball? I am a writer, not a baseball analyst. Sure, I can write about fluffy baseball topics, like spitting, funny baseball nicknames or a 101-year-old Yankee fan (see stories), but the stats, strategy and who's returning to the lineup from the disabled list? That's Ken's specialty.

When he's on the road and I'm home in Baltimore, people see "Suzanne" at the grocery store, gym or church, but they're thinking "Ken" as their baseball rambling begins.

It's Ken they really want when an Oriole fan approaches with a comment that they want Ken back as a player. It's Ken they really want when they ask if I think he will some day broadcast for his "home" team. And, it's Ken they want when they ask me what he thinks of a current hot baseball topic, or if the Yankees will win the pennant. It is also Ken whom they want when someone emails to say she has been thinking about me, yet her next sentence includes the word baseball. (Perhaps it was too awkward to admit she was thinking about someone else's husband?)

There's a difference: I'm 5-foot-7 with long curls holding a pen; Ken is 6-foot-4 with short black hair holding a YES Network microphone.

It's Ken they really want when I walk into a friend's house for a cookout and her husband is looking behind me with the immediate question on his barbeque-stained lips, "Where's Ken?" – as if I'm hiding him in my handbag.

Around the end of summer and the impending close of baseball season, I admit I get a little cranky (can you tell?). Don't get me wrong – I want the Yankees to keep winning, yet I also want my husband to return home from being on and off the road since spring training. Mostly, I feel a tad drained with people talking baseball – to me – when it's Ken they really want.

Sometimes a kind soul will ask if I'm ready for the baseball season to be over. Thank you, and yes I am. But in general, I don't want to talk baseball. Especially in September. It makes me cranky.

Friendly golf foursomes

Strangers' grins peer out from a collection of photos scattered around Ken's office: some buried under paper piles, some stuck in drawers, others graduated to frames or sitting on a crowded credenza among baseball memorabilia.

These are the standard four-golfer poses, a typical souvenir from the bazillion charity golf tournaments in which Ken has been invited to play by his teammates.

The other three golfers in each pose took home an identical photo. I would wager to say they would be able to name Ken in the picture for a long while. But if Ken had to name them, most likely he could not. With no offense to anyone (I can guarantee my husband certainly enjoyed each tournament), Ken has greeted thousands upon thousands of fans over two baseball careers. If he still remembered each of their names, we would change his name to Einstein.

Hopefully, their memory of a day on the links with a baseball celebrity is a great one. Maybe they bragged to their golf buddies that Ken Singleton played in their foursome. Maybe they proudly showed the souvenir photo to a spouse or displayed it on a desk.

And just because Ken may not remember names and faces of the myriad of golfers with whom he shared 18 holes, it doesn't mean he was not congenial and polite while interacting with them. Ken is a very friendly guy.

The one thing he prefers fans "take away" from him is that he looked them in the eye, gave them his time, and tried his best to provide a pleasant experience. Many fans approach or email me (or shared on the *Mrs. Singy* blog) with wonderful comments about the "great guy" I'm married to. He has been described as personable, genuine, hospitable and gracious. And it's true. I have never seen my husband act anything other than gracious to baseball fans.

Our son Dante experienced a good example of this when he met Derek Jeter: "I'll never forget meeting Derek Jeter before a game at Yankee Stadium. What a moment! My dad, always respecting the big names in baseball, informed me, 'It's Mr. Jeter to you,' which Derek laughed off and said, 'Nah, I'm not that old.'

About a month or so later I went with my dad to the game he was working in D.C. against the Nationals. I was on the field near the dugout and Dad was to the side talking to one of the Nationals coaches. Jeter stood about 10 yards in front of me talking to another player. He then turned around in my direction and waved, sort of like, 'What's up, bud?' I had to check to make sure no one else was around me, because I couldn't believe he was talking to me! He remembered who I was without me being next to my dad, which was usually the case with others. That was such a cool moment for me."

Lesson here for all of us is that we cannot control another person's experience, memory, or judgment about another human being. Yet if we are involved in the interaction, what we can control is ourselves. We can do our best to ensure that another person takes away the best pieces of ourselves that we have to offer.

"We grew up down the street from the old stadium on 33rd Street. We would walk to the games or sit in the back yard and listen to the crowds roar. Ken Singleton was one of the greats. I grew up watching baseball with my dad 'Mugs' and my two brothers; I now have a husband and two sons. Baseball and the Orioles have been a huge part of our lives."

- Gayle Mugavero, Orioles fan

3RD INNING

Baltimore & the O's, Hon

The Earl of Baltimore

Unpacking my suitcase on a Sunday morning in January 2013 after Ken and I had returned from a cruise the evening before, I imagined how Marianna Weaver must have felt aboard the cruise ship on which her husband, Earl Weaver, had died two days prior.

I imagined her packing up his clothes and belongings, enduring one more day at sea before their ship docked back in the states, knowing her husband was not in their stateroom but in the ship's morgue. The distraught Marianna then had to disembark the cruise liner, this time not on the arm of her famed once-manager of the Baltimore Orioles, but clutching onto the friends who had no doubt supported her through the shocking ordeal. I thought about how a ruined vacation – and Earl's death – was not in the plan.

On our separate Baltimore Baseball Cruise, a fellow cruiser had approached our breakfast table to whisper in Ken's ear, "Earl Weaver has died." From that point on, Ken's cell phone jingled with calls from reporters and fellow teammates who wanted to discuss the great legend: a manager whose job was to win games; a manager who focused on one game at a time; and one who wasn't afraid to let his players know they screwed up. This manager in a white and orange Orioles uniform didn't like umpires and didn't care if all of Baltimore saw him on television kick up dirt in a huff after a muffed call. Earl was tossed out of 97 games in his career. He was once quoted as saying, "On my tombstone just write, 'The sorest loser that ever lived.'"

And although baseball sometimes didn't bring out the best in him via his obvious tantrums, Earl was "a manager who brought out the best in his players," said Ken, who played on Weaver's team from 1975–1982. "His best attribute was his ability to get us focused. We knew what our jobs were. He made us play hard. I appreciate him today more than I did back then."

Earl had some tremendous players on his roster: Brooks Robinson, Frank Robinson, Cal Ripken Jr., Jim Palmer and Eddie Murray ... all Hall of Famers. Earl was in the Hall of Fame himself, inducted in 1996.

If there's a blessing in everything as they say, then the blessing of Earl's untimely death aboard an Orioles baseball cruise was that he 'went out' having a grand time – partying, laughing and surrounded by baseball fans who adored him. He and Marianna had participated in that annual cruise for some 20 years, joined by several former Orioles players who have changed faces over the years.

Facebook friends and Baltimoreans covered social media with their memories and fond thoughts on the Baltimore legend. Everyone loved the 'Earl of Baltimore' – even if he yelled.

We had grown up watching Earl – a feisty little guy with a cute little face that reminded me of Curious George.

Ken has a horde of humorous stories about Earl. But it wasn't the time to share them. It was a time to honor the man who led Ken and his teammates – a manager who taught, led, inspired and drove them – and won.

The last time Ken spoke to Weaver was at Eddie Murray's statue unveiling the previous summer at Oriole Park at Camden Yards. "He and I were alone," Ken said. "He said he appreciated how hard I had played for him. But it was Earl who brought out the best in me. To say that he was unique is an understatement. There will never be another manager like him. Rest in peace, Earl."

The late Earl Weaver, Orioles manager 1968–1982 (Singleton photo)

Bling of the ring: a World Series bonus

1983 Baltimore Orioles World Series ring

When he looks at his ring, Ken sees "an effort by at least 25 players. That particular year there was no team better," Ken said. "This is why every player goes out there every season – to win the World Series. It's a tremendous feeling of accomplishment to look at the ring. That's forever."

Irreplaceable, special and meaningful, yes. But the O's 10-carat gold ring is not as impressive in diamonds and gold as the Yankees' rings, and certainly not as glitzy. However, it is older and over the years the design of championship rings have become larger and more flamboyant.

A bed of 18 small diamonds (.75 carats) sits under the word ORIOLES in script. WORLD CHAMPIONS 1983 surrounds that. One side reads SINGLETON with Ken's No. 29 under a World Series trophy; the other side reads WORLD SERIES 1983 with the cartoon-bird Oriole logo swinging a bat and wearing a gold crown.

Ken owns four World Series rings, one earned as a player (1983) and three gifted as a TV broadcaster for the New York Yankees when they were World Champions in 1998, 1999 and 2009. There is no doubt as to which ring Ken feels most proud to wear. (Singleton photo)

Surely that's how the team must have felt – like kings – when the last out was made in 1983 in Game 5 of the World Series versus the Phillies in Philadelphia. It was a year to remember by the ring on the finger. That year each Oriole received $64,000 after winning the championship.

Comparatively, today's players are awarded about $350,000. "That money's gone," Ken said, "but the ring lives on."

1998 New York Yankees World Series ring

"It was very kind of the Yankees to present me with the World Series rings," said Ken who received them as an announcer after three of their champion seasons. "I will cherish them forever."

In two wooden boxes with oval Plexiglas tops are etched the words NEW YORK YANKEES WORLD CHAMPIONS. One reads 1998; the other 1999. A third smaller two-toned cherrywood box (pictured) is engraved with WORLD CHAMPIONS NY 2009 and houses that year's ring. These extraordinary pieces of jewelry are extremely rare, owned by few.

Gently lift the lid of the first box and view a treasure snuggled into a deep slit in the dark Yankee blue velvet. An impressive NY lined with diamonds is smack in the middle of this ring, a luminescent blue background lifting the logo surrounded by an oval of 24 diamonds representing the number of World Series championships. Around that in a larger oval are 3-D block letters spelling WORLD CHAMPIONS, and the year split into a 19 and a 98 on either side.

One side of the 14-carat gold ring reads 125-50 (wins/losses in "a great year," Ken said) over a Yankees logo with the words BEST EVER engraved underneath. The other side boldly reveals SINGLETON over a tiny Yankee Stadium in the background. Over it is a 3-D World Series trophy and the word TRADITION underneath.

1999 New York Yankees World Series ring

More impressive than the contents of the first box is the brilliance of the 1999 need-sunglasses-to-view ring, its 3-D NY logo spelled out in lines of diamonds and positioned on a thin NY-shaped blue background. This logo ensemble is perched boldly on a field of tinier diamonds hard to count with the naked eye. The ring's border holds 26 more diamonds with the year split into a 19 and a *99*.

Spin the ring to the left and the intricate detail reveals the Yankees top hat and bat logo with the inscription THE CENTURY'S TEAM and YANKEES. Below that are the façades of the old and new Yankee Stadiums. Under it is a gold 25th WORLD CHAMPIONSHIP. Spin the ring another half circle and SINGLETON is engraved in caps. Under the surname is a tiny piece of the stadium etched with a New York skyline beyond it, the twin towers clearly identifiable. Atop that on this bulky substantial ring are the recognized World

Series trophy and another 25th on top of it. Underneath is a simple and meaningful word: TRADITION.

2009 New York Yankees World Series ring

A third Yankees ring gifted to Ken is that of the 2009 World Series win. If possible, this ring's 14-carat white gold bling is even blingier than the previous two. Its façade is entirely set with diamonds comprising the initials NY sitting atop an all-diamond baseball diamond (that's a lot of diamond talk). That cluster sits atop two borders of diamonds around the ring.

Twist the ring to the right and SINGLETON is engraved in 3-D lettering. Under Ken's surname is the circular Yankees baseball bat and top hat logo. Under that is the word TRADITION. Spin the ring the other way and it reads WORLD CHAMPIONS; under that is a replica of Yankee Stadium and along the bottom it says 2009 UNITY.

Finally, stamped inside the ring in a circular design are the words: YANKEE STADIUM 2009 INAUGURAL SEASON. In the middle is a flag flying above the façade of Yankee Stadium.

Although Ken is extremely honored to own these three beautiful New York Yankees rings, the piece of jewelry generally resting on his right hand ring finger – his 1983 World Series ring – is the one he earned as a Baltimore Oriole and the one for which he feels the most pride. It is an icon that depicts the dream of every Major Leaguer – being a World Champion.

Ken shows three of his four World Series rings. (Singleton photo)

Torn between pinstripes and birds?

When the Yankees play in Baltimore, Ken is in "commute mode," able to zip down I-83 to Camden Yards from our home in Baltimore County. This is welcome and different, as he is normally hopping a plane or a train to meet up with the Yankees and the YES Network crew.

Because he wore an Oriole uniform for 10 seasons (1975-84), and now announces games for the pinstripes, fans generally think he must be "torn" between his allegiances. Mrs. Singy sat down with Ken to get the real score.

Mrs. Singy: What is it like for you to announce a Yankees/Orioles game?
Ken: Much like all of the others, that's the way I look at it. I approach it the same way. I think other people may look at it differently because I used to play for the Orioles and I've been with the Yankees so long. Maybe they think, "He must be torn." I'm not really. I just do the games. And my job is easier when the Yankees win. I've been fortunate to see them win quite a bit.

Mrs. Singy: Would you prefer to announce a Yankees/Orioles game in Baltimore or New York?
Ken: Well, I like doing Yankees games in Baltimore because I don't have to travel far. I've lived here for about 40 years. But I really love Yankee Stadium. I don't think there is a more exciting stadium in the Major Leagues in terms of the crowd, how the fans get into the team, and their knowledge of the game. Plus, New York is where I grew up [Mount Vernon]. I will always love New York City.

Mrs. Singy: When you announce Yankee games in Baltimore, does it bring back memories, or perhaps not since you didn't play in Camden Yards?
Ken: Not so much; only when I'm reminded by people who I might see around the stadium whom I've known over the years, like Jim Palmer, [the late] Mike Flanagan, and some of the ushers who have carried over from Memorial Stadium to Camden Yards. But that was a long time ago. Times change. Camden Yards has a different atmosphere than Memorial Stadium. A lot of that has to do with the fact that the Orioles were big winners in those days.

Mrs. Singy: What do you say when fans consistently ask why you don't announce for Baltimore?
Ken: I consider myself a Yankees broadcaster; I work in New York. I'm very happy where I am. Who wouldn't be happy working for a team that I have witnessed win the World Series four times? I've seen them in the playoffs more than a dozen times. When I was announcing games for the Montreal Expos, fans in Baltimore didn't seem to mind. Now that I do games for New York, at first they would ask, "How can you do that?" But I think now they understand better … I hope. The Yankees are good. They are a good team to work for.

Mrs. Singy: What did you think of the NY Yankees when you were an Oriole?
Ken: Good question. I had a lot of respect for the Yankees. They were the team that we always tried to beat. As Orioles, we went to the World Series twice and I can recall in 10 years in Baltimore, we finished second, six times – some of those to the Yankees. They had great players: Thurman Munson, Reggie Jackson, Willie Randolph, Ron Guidry, Catfish Hunter and Lou Piniella. George Steinbrenner was still the boss back then. I had a lot of respect for their organization.

Mrs. Singy: What are your responses to these questions from Baltimore fans? *Do you still have orange and black running through your blood? We need you back on the Orioles! Why don't you live in NY? Do you miss playing?*
Ken: When they comment that they need me back, I say, "There was a time." But those days are over. It's very nice for people to remember, but the game goes on and the players change. About living in New York … that's easy. All I have to do is get on a train and I'm there – it's a simple commute. My kids grew up here in Baltimore, you [Mrs. Singy] are from here. I don't miss playing, no. Like I said, those days are over. When you start as a player, you know you can't play forever. I was blessed to have played for 15 years – 12 on winning teams. Fifteen years in the Majors is a good run. I earned a good living – still earn a good living. I've been in the Majors for close to 50 years now.

Mrs. Singy: What do you think about today's Orioles?
Ken: They are a contender in the American League East. They have a chance. Buck Showalter has done a remarkable job since he's taken over as manager. They've been in the playoffs two of the last four seasons.

Crabs, California and Eddie's wedding

Picking Maryland steamed crabs is a messy endeavor. You either know how to do it or you don't. So only veteran crab eaters would think it odd wearing surgical gloves while picking crabs – in California no less. Yet this is what a small group of friends did on the night before Eddie Murray's wedding in the condo of Brady Anderson and Rene Gonzales, both former Orioles. It was 1993.

I had flown out to California with my friend Diane Hock to attend the Murray wedding, and she had promised steamed crabs to Brady, Rene and friends. After carting them to the airport in a large box packed with dry ice, Diane successfully delivered the seafood securely to the dining room table in Huntington Beach where the Californians gobbled garishly with nary a speck of Old Bay seasoning on anyone's fingers. When folks began to snap on white surgical gloves to operate on the crustaceans, I almost spit out a mouthful of Coors Light. Indeed, a funny sight to behold.

Not as funny as the small prank played on me the next day at the wedding. A guy at our table convinced me to ask the sturdy man at the next table for an autograph, claiming it was Barry Bonds.

"I'm not Barry Bonds," the guy answered. Oh. Oops.

"Very sorry to have bothered you," I said, red-faced with daggers in my eyes directed at the trickster.

I've never repeated that mistake. (At least I knew what Eddie looked like.)

The Murray wedding was a splendid event. I remember many pink, red and white balloons decorating the hall and meeting Eddie's clan of siblings (he has 11). Somewhere on an old VHS tape is a long silly rhyming verse, which a small group of us had concocted during the reception for the videographer as our congratulatory message for the bride and groom. High on wine and the wedding atmosphere, we giggled hysterically during our "performance" and had quite amused ourselves in the creative process of writing it.

Post reception, we had been invited back to Eddie's house in Santa Clarita for a party. What a colossal structure! A Swiss Chalet style that could have been featured in a home and garden magazine. It hosted a ridiculous amount of bathrooms (11! Did Eddie build one for each sibling?); nine bedrooms; a wine cellar; bridal suite; nine-car garage; elevator; cave room;

an adorable little girl's room with a ladder leading to a loft; a dream kitchen; and an enormous recreation room with a billiards table. Eddie's collection of baseball hats hung on the wall.

Even the glass and wood design of the front door was beautiful. The square footage went on forever. In a 35-foot lake in the front of the house – stocked with large fish – a beautiful swan paddled around softly (or did I dream it?) and peacocks wandered the grounds.

Ken and I had visited Eddie's house one other time, after a Dodgers-Expos game. We followed him home to visit, and upon leaving, shook our heads in awe all the way back to Baltimore. Eddie eventually sold the house and is no longer married.

Ken and Eddie are good friends and bump into each other at various stadiums, baseball events and golf tournaments. Eddie is often in Baltimore, sometimes to attend an Orioles-related function, and certainly, to eat Maryland steamed crabs.

Once a popular Baltimore Oriole, ***Brady Anderson*** *(left) enjoys Baltimore crabs with friends in his California home the night before Eddie Murray's wedding in 1993. On Mrs. Singy's right (seated holding crab) is* ***Rene Gonzales,*** *also a previous Oriole****. Diane Hock*** *is far right. (Singleton photo)*

Chris Singleton is not our kid

At the time of this blog entry, this was the second baseball season our then 30-year-old son, Justin, had not played since he wore diapers. Although he batted and fielded his way effectively up to Triple A in the Toronto Blue Jays system, Justin opted to move on to the next phase of his life.

When Justin played in the minors, another kid named Singleton played in the majors – *Chris Singleton*. Ken and I constantly fought off the rumor that Chris was our son; there is no relation. Fans automatically launched into the conversation, "I saw your son do this-and-that on the field" and we repeatedly answered, “Chris Singleton is not our son – *Justin* Singleton is!”

An honest mistake considering Ken and Chris shared the same name and No. 29. The rumor rolled along further during the one season Chris played for the Baltimore Orioles.

Yet the biggest blunder was a promotional flier once printed by Topps Sports depicting side-by-side baseball cards of father/son Major Leaguers. On it they included cards of Ken and Chris. (This didn't help the rumor.) I wrote to Topps to clear it up but never received a response.

I'm sure Chris Singleton is a terrific guy, yet we are not his parents. Our pride is with Justin. In his successful baseball career, Justin was deserving of his own recognition, and being connected to his big league father.

The name jumble doesn't matter any longer now that the boys have moved along with their respective careers. Yet just in case anyone out there still connects Chris' name to Ken's, I thought I'd clear up the rumor ... Chris Singleton is not our kid.

(next page) ***Justin Singleton*** *signed as a non-drafted free agent with the Toronto Blue Jays in 2001 after his junior year at Clemson University. As an outfielder, he spent six seasons in the Blue Jays' system, including two at AAA Syracuse. Justin also played one season of independent ball with the Camden Riversharks and York Revolution of the Atlantic League. Contrary to rumor, former Major Leaguer* ***Chris Singleton*** *is not related to Ken. (Photo courtesy Steve Moore)*

Just hanging on a fence watching a World Series parade

Everything in New York City seems to be done on a grand scale. The newspapers said an estimated two million people lined the streets to celebrate the Yankees' World Series win in 2009. Two million! We were just two people; Ken and me, watching it on television at home in Maryland.

"I enjoyed watching the city's reaction to winning the championship," said Ken, "because they haven't had one in nine years. I also liked hearing what the players had to say, like CC Sabathia's comment, 'There's nothing like winning in New York!' "

At the time, Ken was delighted for the players able to experience such a conquest in their first year with the Yankees, such as Sabathia, Mark Teixeira and A.J. Burnett.

No doubt watching the festivities elicited his own happy memories as a Baltimore Oriole during a victorious time in 1983 after the Birds had clinched the World Series (upsetting the Phillies). In Baltimore City's World Series parade, Ken and his previous wife, Colette, and the two boys at ages 4 and 7, sat in the back of a convertible Oldsmobile.

On a much smaller scale than the parade in New York, Ken remembers, "People got very close to the convertibles carrying the players. They were able to touch us – that wouldn't happen nowadays. My two young boys were in the car. Justin didn't like it. He said the fans were too close. It made him uncomfortable and I didn't like that he felt that way."

"That was a big celebration!" said Matthew Singleton, now 39. "I was in the car with Dad during the parade. It was fun! I enjoyed the ride."

As a fan in the throng of that boisterous scenario on "Oriole Boulevard" near Fayette Street, there was only one place for me to go for a better view – up. Together, my friend Susan Comotto and I braved the crowd in our Orioles caps and corporate clothes to watch the convoy. In a dress and a skirt, we somehow climbed up onto a thin ledge and daringly hung onto a fence to catch clearer glimpses of the titillating celebration over the hairy heads of the other zillion fans.

Hand-to-hand between us was a small stuffed Oriole mascot. The ballplayers and their families shook hands, accepted pats on the backs, and grinned in the hype of an overwhelming reception from the deafening and massive crowd. It is a great memory.

I was an average Orioles fan like the rest of the screaming people showing pride for our home team. Had someone told me that October day that one Mr. Ken Singleton passing by to the shouts of "Singy!" and "C'mon Ken, hit it in the bullpen!" would one day be my husband, I would have laughed at the notion and probably fallen off the ledge.

"It was fun," said Ken, who remembers that people were hanging off street poles and out of office windows. At age 36 and ready to wrap up a long and productive baseball career, it had taken him 13 seasons before he had the opportunity to play on a World Championship team.

"Winning the Series was such a feeling of accomplishment," he said. "For that particular season no team played better than us. We went down in history for champions of that year."

Gleefully, the Orioles had returned to Memorial Stadium on 33rd Street by bus from Philly after the Series finished. Ken remembers that "the fans had been waiting for us – they were all over the place, in the parking lot and everywhere, in spite of it being close to midnight. There were so many people cheering us on, it was hard to drive through the streets."

Since then, the Orioles have hosted several World Series Reunions at Oriole Park at Camden Yards, holding onto that precious era. Ken and many of his former teammates have been invited back to reminisce.

"I'm sure Cal Ripken thought he would be on many more championships teams," Ken said. Cal was then in his second season as an Oriole. "But it never happened again. It's been 33 years."

Hubby wears his World Series ring proudly and often. "Winning was the culmination of a good year," he said.

(previous) ***Ken*** *with his family in the 1983 World Series parade through the streets of Baltimore City.*

(left) ***Suzanne Molino*** *on right before she knew Ken, with then sister-in-law* ***Susan Comotto*** *as they watched the Orioles parade on "Oriole Blvd" (below).*

(Singleton photos)

Before Ken: Clean confessions of an Oriole fan turned baseball wife

As Ken and I celebrate our 25th year of marriage in 2016, I couldn't help but reminisce about "once upon a baseball time" before meeting him:

• Once upon a baseball time I forced myself to slurp raw oysters (which I loathe) with Brooks Robinson (whom I adore) at a fundraiser held at The Cloisters Museum in Baltimore while I worked for a video production company. I had interviewed Brooks for the party video we were taping. I still hate raw oysters; I still adore Brooks.

• Once upon a baseball time I was an ordinary fan in the upper deck of Memorial Stadium screaming along with the other 52,000 beer-filled fans, "*C'mon Ken! Hit it in the bullpen!*" and watching Wild Bill Hagy spell out O-R-I-O-L-E-S. Today we own a seat from Memorial Stadium that sits in our house painted with those very words.

• Once upon a baseball time a friend named Bob pretended he was Oriole Rich Dauer as we exited a Memorial Stadium game long after the game had ended. Fans waiting outside for players' autographs surrounded him because another friend in our group had shouted, "Hey, it's Rich Dauer!" Stupidly, Bob signed their programs and balls. I cringed thinking how they believed the authenticity of the situation and thought that Bob was a goober for tricking them.

• Once upon a baseball time in my early 20s at Memorial Stadium, a friend and I slid from top to bottom of the long metal partition between escalators. I sported the largest, deepest purplish bruise ever known to skin (top of left hip to outside of left knee) as my body thumped solidly against the base at the bottom of the escalators. Luckily, I had consumed several stadium beers that helped mask the pain of the impact as I giggled from the ride. (The next day, however, I was crying in pain.)

• Once upon a baseball time during lunch hour while working in downtown Baltimore, I stood in a long line at a player appearance to meet Eddie Murray and Cal Ripken Jr.; I walked away smiling with an Eddie autograph and a Cal kiss.

• Once upon a baseball time I chatted with Cal Ripken Jr. at Christopher's nightclub when he first played for the Orioles – before I knew him through Ken and before he was very famous.

• Once upon a baseball time in 1985 when I worked in the corporate world at Maryland National Bank, I interviewed Ken for our company newspaper when he played for the Orioles. He was our company's spokesman for a product called The Lineup. I still have that newspaper. And I still have Ken.

(above) After waiting in a long line at a player appearance in downtown Baltimore, Suzanne (before she became Mrs. Singy) leans in for a smooch with ***Cal Ripken Jr.*** *in 1984..*

Eddie Murray's *autograph from this same event.*

(Singleton photos)

The night Tom Selleck missed meeting Mamma Gina

This is an older story but a favorite. Twenty years later, my non-baseball-fan mamma, Gina, still regrets declining a game ticket after Ken and I had invited my parents to Cal Ripken Jr.'s 2131 grand event Sept. 5-6, 1995 at Oriole Park. Mamma Gina didn't quite understand the great hoopla created around such baseball milestones. She ended up missing out on meeting one of her favorite actors, Tom Selleck.

Sept. 5 was the tie of Lou Gehrig's consecutive game record; Sept. 6 was the night Cal broke that record. For each of those games, Ken was given six tickets. For the first game, my dad, Louie, and my sister Pamela joined us, as did our then 16-year-old son Justin and his girlfriend Michele. Mom had agreed to babysit our then 3-year-old son Dante at our house.

Before the game, the Orioles hosted a fabulous VIP party with some big batters in attendance: Tom Selleck, Johnny Unitas, basketball pro David "The Admiral" Robinson, *The Young & The Restless* soap opera star Don Diamont, Frank Robinson, Hank Aaron, Ernie Banks, the late Earl Weaver, Olympics speed skater Bonnie Blair and other sports-related greats. It was a thrilling and memorable evening!

When I phoned Mom to check on the tot, she was frazzled. It was one of those nights … "I want Mommy and Daddy!" Dante had been crying "plenty loud," she said, since we left, and Mom-Mom was unable to console him. Worse, he had glimpsed Ken on television at the stadium, retrieved our car keys, and demanded that his grandmother drive him there.

It was a night of *Babysitting Hell.*

Adding to my mother's misery, I mistakenly mentioned, "Guess who's here? Guess who we met? Tom Selleck!" to which my mother's wail could have been heard from our Baltimore County home all the way downtown. She adores Tom Selleck, who doesn't?

"Do you mean I gave up a chance to meet Tom Selleck for this?" She was in disbelief that she was stuck at home all evening trying to calm an irritable toddler while her daughters and her husband hobnobbed with Hollywood.

Sorry Tom, but you missed meeting a very pleasant lady – and a great babysitter. Thankfully, being the sweet Mom-Mom she is, it wasn't the last time she agreed to watch our kids. Thanks, Mamma.

*Actor **Tom Selleck**, **Louie Molino** (Ken's father-in-law) and **Mrs. Singy** at Cal Ripken Jr.'s 2131 events at Oriole Park at Camden Yards (September 1995). The late **Johnny Unitas** is pictured right. Sports pros and Hollywood stars were Cal's guests that evening at a VIP reception in the visiting clubhouse. (Singleton photo)*

4th INNING

Inside the Singletons' Photo Album

Ken Singleton Celebrity Golf Classic 2010 at Hunt Valley Country Club: ***Boog Powell*** *and* ***Mrs. Singy***

(below) At same tournament, the late ***Paul Blair, Ken Singleton*** *and* ***Jim Palmer***

(Singleton photos)

***Brady Anderson** and **Ken Singleton** in Cooperstown Hall of Fame Museum 2007.*
*(below) **Scott McGregor, Ken, Gary Roenicke, Rich Dauer** at Oriole Park. (Singleton photos)*

Ross & Byrd Grimsley *with* ***Suzanne & Ken Singleton*** *on Baltimore Baseball Cruise.*
(below) ***Ken & Suzanne*** *with* ***Carol & Tippy Martinez*** *on cruise.(Singleton photos)*

Ken *and his former broadcast partner and friend,* **Dave Van Horne**, *before a Montreal Expos game in Dodger Stadium 1990. Dave currently announces radio games for the Florida Marlins. (below) Orioles locker room at Memorial Stadium. (Singleton photos)*

***Eddie Murray, Dennis & Luz Martinez, Carol & Tippy Martinez** poolside at the Singletons during a Cool Kids Campaign crab feast 2014, part of the Ken Singleton Celebrity Golf Classic.*
***Ken** in background with son **Dante** and former pitcher **Dave Johnson**.*
*(below) **Mrs. Singy** with **Eddie Murray** in Cooperstown Hall of Fame Museum 2007 (Singleton photos)*

During an Orioles lawn party in Cooperstown, ***Cal Ripken Jr*** *and* ***Eddie Murray*** *greet the littlest Singleton as* ***Ken*** *looks on. Cal was being inducted into the Hall of Fame along with* ***Tony Gwynn****, July 2007. (Singleton photo)*

*In 1984, the Baltimore Orioles were invited to The White House in Washington, D.C. for a Little League celebration. Ken and **Rick Dempsey** stand near **President Ronald Reagan** (seated) as he signs a declaration honoring Little League Day. **Jim Palmer** is partially pictured left, behind **Vice President George Bush.***

(Photo courtesy Ronald Reagan Library)

***Ken** shakes hands with **Vice President Bush**, standing next to **President Reagan. Rick Dempsey** is in front of Ken; **Joe Altobelli** is in background (touching hat).*

*(next page) **Ken** chats with **Vice President Bush** at a Little League game on the White House lawn. Seated to right of **President Reagan** with glove in hand is **Scott McGregor** and two Little League players.*

(Photos courtesy Ronald Reagan Library)

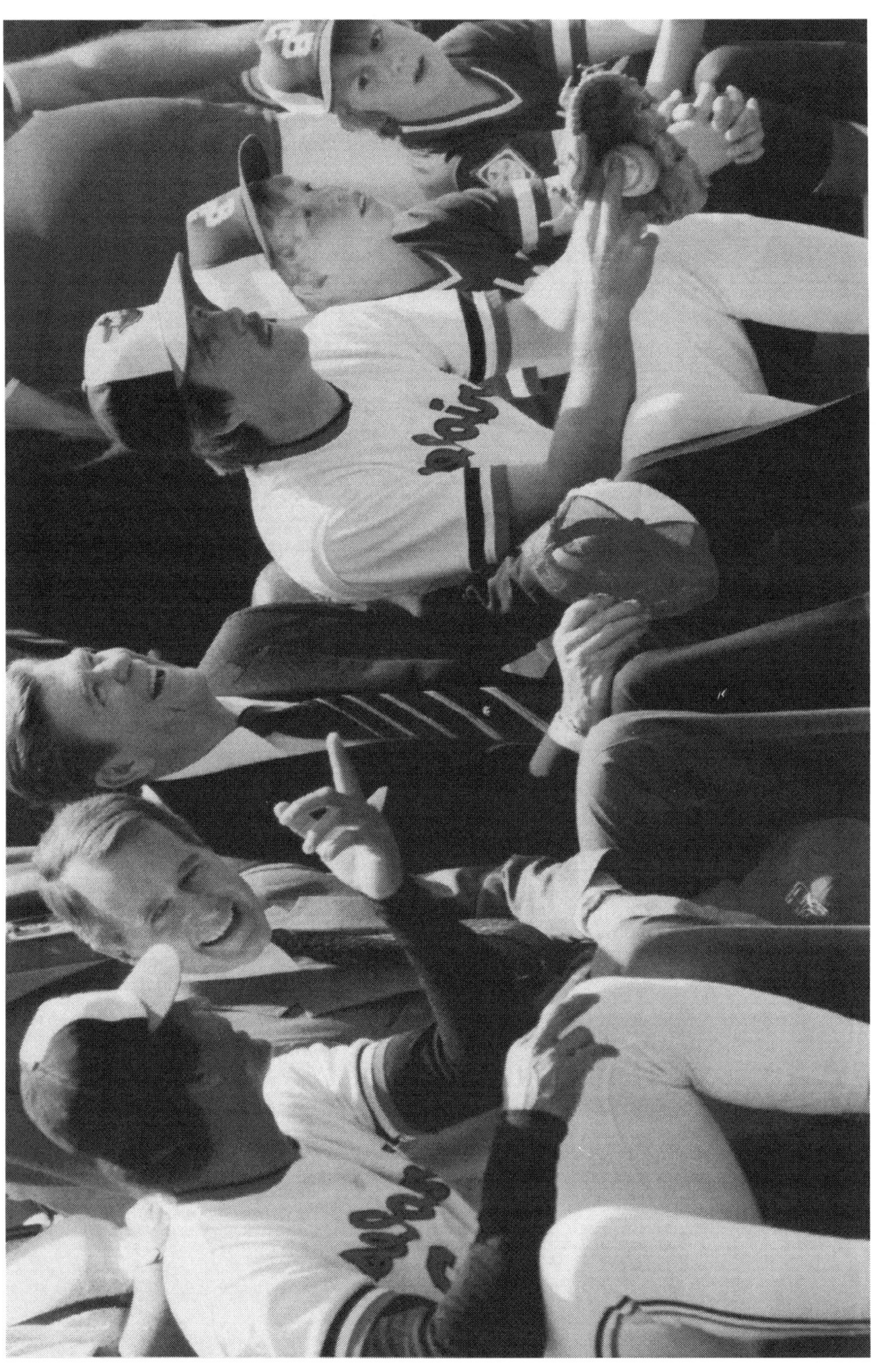

Ken
Singleton

*(previous) Suzanne & Ken with kids and Ken's mom, the late **Lucille Singleton**, at Sports Legends Museum which had created displays for various Orioles, including Ken. The museum has since closed.*

*(below) Managua, Nicaragua 2015: **Eddie Murray, Scott McGregor, Dennis Martinez, Ken Singleton** during Dennis' charity golf tournament to benefit kids with cancer.*

(Singleton photos)

***Mrs. Singy** with actor **Kevin Costner** in Dodger Stadium before a 'Hollywood Stars Game' 1990; (below) Retired Orioles **Scott McGregor** and **Ken** are still close friends, 2015 (Singleton photos)*

(previous) Ken's agent, ***Ron Shapiro,*** *with* ***Doug DeCinces*** *and* ***Cal Ripken Jr****. during Cal's Hall of Fame Induction Weekend in Cooperstown, N.Y. 2007.*

Sports agent ***Ron Shapiro*** *(with Ken below) founded the sports marketing firm Shapiro, Robinson & Associates in 1976, and is also a best selling author, civic leader, educator, and attorney. He has represented Ken during both baseball careers: with the Orioles and currently as a NY Yankees broadcaster. Shapiro has represented some impressive names in baseball including more Hall of Famers than any other sports agent, to name a few: Cal Ripken Jr, Jim Palmer, Brooks Robinson, Kirby Puckett and Eddie Murray. USA Today called Ron Shapiro "one of baseball's most respected agent-attorneys."*

(Singleton photos)

***Singy** at Oriole Park at Camden Yards in Baltimore, where his plaque hangs among those in the Orioles Hall of Fame.*

*(next page) **Singy** at Steinbrenner Stadium in Tampa, home of NY Yankees spring training. (Singleton photos)*

Time World Champions
42
MARIANO RIVERA
NY

Singy *with one of his favorites, the late* ***Yogi Berra,***
in front of Tony Gwynn's Hall of Fall display in Cooperstown 2007
(Singleton photo)

Ken has been in baseball for close to 50 years in two careers and has announced New York Yankees games on YES Network for 15 of those years; previously for MSG/Madison Square Garden. (Photo courtesy E.H. Wallop/YES Network)

*Ken pitches to **Matt Singleton** in Memorial Stadium as he holds toddler **Justin**. The boys are now 36 and 39. (below) Ken & Suzanne with the two youngest Singletons, now ages 19 and 24. (Singleton photos)*

(previous) ***Ken & Suzanne****, New York City 2015*

(above) NYY Steak restaurant in Manhattan displays a series of engraved steak knives representing New York Yankees and broadcasters. Its décor is Yankees everything, right down to the wait staff wearing pinstripes.

(below) Ken and ***Johnny Unitas*** *often sat together to watch their sons' basketball games.* ***Justin Singleton*** *and* ***Chad Unitas*** *attended St. Paul School for Boys from kindergarten through 12th grade and remain close friends. (Singleton photos)*

The late ***Mike Flanagan, Ross Grimsley, Ken*** *and their friend,* ***Jimmy Neukum,*** *at the Singletons' wedding 1991. (below)* ***Cal Ripken Jr., Jim Palmer, Brooks Robinson*** *and the late* ***Earl Weaver*** *at* ***Eddie Murray'****s bronze statue unveiling at Oriole Park August 2012. Singy is behind them (to left) as is Buck Showalter (in uniform) and Brady Anderson behind Earl.*

(next page) Yankee Stadium opener 2009 (Singleton photos)

WEATHERPROOF
WEATHERPROOF

*The youngest Singleton in 2007 with **Derek Jeter**, retired NY Yankee, in the workout room at Camden Yards in Baltimore. (below) **Dante Singleton** with retired Orioles **Eddie Murray** and **Bill Swaggerty** poolside at the Singletons VIP party during the Ken Singleton Celebrity Golf Classic (Singleton photos)*

(l-r) Orioles ***Brooks Robinson****,* ***Tommy Davis, Ken Singleton*** *and* ***Elrod Hendricks*** *head for the dugout after Davis knocked a grand slam home run in the 5th inning for an O's win in 1975. (UPI photo)*

*Two of the Singleton kids with comedian **Seth Myers** after a taping of Center Stage in New York City. Center Stage is hosted by **Michael Kay**, one of Ken's broadcast partners. (Singleton photo)*

Ken Singleton (photo courtesy Baltimore Orioles)

*Ken's mother **Lucille Singleton** snapped these photos when the Orioles won the 1983 American League Championship.*

(Singleton photos)

Lucille and Joe Singleton with sons Fred and Ken 2005 (Singleton photo)

"As my pitch sailed over the roof of our parents' house in Mount Vernon, N.Y., in the early 1960s, it became evident that two paths were being forged into the future: the first being that Ken could hit a baseball like a major leaguer; the second being I couldn't throw a ball like one.

Some nine years later, confirmation of both projected paths had come true as Ken made his Major League debut as a New York Met against the Chicago Cubs on June 24, 1970.

Watching my big brother play in the majors has been one of the greatest thrills of my life, with the ultimate joy reached in Philadelphia on October 16, 1983 as the Orioles defeated the Phillies to win the World Series. Watching Ken and his teammates celebrate on the field made my family – and Oriole fans around the nation – proud. I felt as much pride then as I had in the backyard years earlier when I was able to sneak a fastball by Kenny for a called strike three." **- J. Frederick Singleton**

5th INNING

The Emotional Side of Baseball

Farewell, Flanny

We don't think much about never seeing someone again when we part ways, matter-of-factly saying, "See you later," because we expect we will.

Ken shook his friend's hand in that same fashion as he and Mike "Flanny" Flanagan parted ways at New York's Penn Station July 31, 2011 after the Orioles played the New York Yankees. The two had shared a ride from the stadium. Ken said, "I'll see you when we get to Baltimore."

"I'll see you when we get to Baltimore," were the last words Ken said to his friend and former teammate, ***Mike Flanagan****, who committed suicide in 2011. The friends are pictured here in Cooperstown, N.Y. 2007 at an Orioles lawn party during Induction Weekend. (Singleton photo)*

It was no different than the way Ken had parted with any baseball friend countless times, knowing their paths would cross soon in the baseball world.

"That was the last time I saw him," said Ken about his former Orioles teammate who took his life August 2011 behind his house in Baltimore County.

Over 14 years, we had passed the Flanagans' historic farmhouse hundreds of times as we drove in and out of our neighborhood 1.5 miles away. And almost every time I looked at their house, I recalled Mike's wife once reporting that she had experienced a few incidents inside of the old house to indicate it was haunted.

That week, ghosts were furthest from my mind as I looked up the hill at their stone house. Instead, I shook my head with sadness about the troubled thoughts and feelings that haunted such a decent, funny and nice man ... feelings awful enough for him to do what no human being ever should do to himself.

Of course Mike's other former teammates – many of them still residing here in Baltimore – reeled from this tragedy, mindful, of course, that none of them were quite as affected as Mike's wife and three daughters.

After returning home from Camden Yards when the Yankees were in town that week, Ken said the mood on the press level was obviously solemn. Where he normally would have bumped into Mike as an Orioles broadcaster, there was no Mike. There was only a group of incredibly sad colleagues missing Flanagan's presence; maybe silently wishing they could have somehow helped their friend before he hurt himself.

"This is not easy," said Ken, of his friend since 1975. "I played with Flanny for 10 years. He was a fantastic teammate, a trusted teammate. Not only was he a good pitcher, he was a good person, and that translated throughout the team."

Before the next game, the Yankees paid tribute to Mike with a moment of silence, showing his photo on the center field scoreboard. The Orioles held a moment of silence in memory, along with a video tribute of him. Mike's uniform No. 46 was posted on the out-of-town scoreboard in right field.

"It was a very nice tribute," Ken said. "Everyone was crying."

Mike shall be missed, yet he is haunted no longer.

Jeter-man Joe: A dying boy's wish

There exists a plethora of Derek Jeter fans and they all want an autographed baseball. One young Baltimore boy didn't have much time left to get one … he was dying from leukemia.

When Chris Federico, president of Cool Kids Campaign (which serves kids with cancer), called Joe Gorman's dad, Gregg Gorman, to ask how young Joe was faring, the bad report told of a relapse – the chemo wasn't taking. Then the six words were uttered that no one wants to hear about a person they love, let alone a kid, "There's nothing more they can do."

"It was hard for Gregg to hold it in," said Chris, who asked him if the Cool Kids Campaign could do anything.

"Well, I know Joe would really like a Ferrari," Gregg joked, even with a broken heart. "Or anything signed by Derek Jeter – or a chance to meet him. But Joe doesn't have much time left."

"I can help with that," said Federico, who had grown to love the kid. "I'll call Ken Singleton."

Ken serves on the board of this organization dedicated to improving the quality of life for pediatric oncology patients – and their families – experiencing the trauma of a cancer diagnosis and treatment.

When Ken learned of the situation, he said, "I'll take care of it," knowing he could ask Jeter to sign a ball when next he saw him at Steinbrenner Field during spring training. Near the batting cages, Ken approached Derek with a practice ball and explained the request from young Joe.

"Sure, I'll sign it," said Jeter, "but get a brand-new one from the equipment manager in the clubhouse." (Derek didn't want to send a dirty ball to Joe.)

On Monday – the day before Joe's birthday – Ken, Chris and Cool Kids Campaign's Executive Director Sharon Perfetti drove to Johns Hopkins Children's Center in downtown Baltimore to deliver the much-desired autograph. Yet Joe was not conscious. His dad had tried to wake him up, "Hey, guess what, Joe? Your wish came true. Derek signed a ball!"

But it was too late. The ball placed in the young man's hands remained for a few minutes, then rolled out.

"I didn't get a chance to talk to him," Ken said when he arrived home. "He wasn't coherent."

Ken, Chris and Sharon had a good visit with Joe's parents and an uncle – "nice people, who were extremely appreciative that Derek and I took the time to get the ball for their son," said Ken. "They were obviously in pain but were upbeat. They knew the situation that Joe wasn't going to be around much longer."

One day after his 15th birthday, Joe died.

Joe Gorman
March 8, 1996 – March 9, 2011

Ken personally had asked for an autographed baseball from ***Derek Jeter*** *to deliver in person to* ***Joe Gorman****, 15, suffering from cancer. Joe died just days later. (Photo courtesy Cool Kids Campaign)*

Peace for Hideki

It's always distressing to hear about a human being making the choice to end his life, and sadder still when it was someone with whom you had once enjoyed an interaction. Hideki Irabu committed suicide July 28, 2011 in his Los Angeles home.

When Hideki was a Yankee, Ken and I once went out to lunch with him and his translator, George Rose, at our favorite sushi restaurant here in Baltimore. Hideki's translator travelled everywhere with him, since the player spoke little English.

The use of a translator is quite an interesting conversation method – a matter of trust in all three parties. As sushi lovers, Ken and I trusted Hideki as well, as we gingerly tasted pieces of eel he had recommended.

Sushi aside, I do not know what dreadful demons Hideki faced that were consuming enough to cause him to find a noose; however, I do know that whatever nationality we are and whichever language we speak ... depression is depression, despair is despair and tragedy is tragedy. There are no words for that in English or Japanese.

"I found that my interactions with Hideki were very interesting," Ken said. "He was an interesting man, not outgoing, just always observing. Everything seemed new to him. For us to have had that lunch with him and his interpreter helped me to view him in a completely different light. That was a nice afternoon."

Ken added that it's sad to see someone give up hope.

To his family, to his friends, to his fans come sympathetic thoughts. We hope Hideki has found his peace.

Cool Kids Campaign established in Mark Belanger's honor

It never seems to be the right order of things when people die before reaching the average human lifespan. Yet sadly, it is sometimes reality.

The nonprofit organization Cool Kids Campaign was cofounded by ***Rob Belanger****, partially established in honor of his father, Baltimore Orioles shortstop,* ***Mark Belanger,*** *who died of lung cancer. (Photo courtesy Baltimore Orioles)*

These were the thoughts of Ken and his former teammates as they bid goodbye to a teammate and friend Mark Belanger – eight-time Rawlings Gold Glove award winner – who died from lung cancer in 1998 at age 54.

Although sometimes God's plans deem a young death for reasons we cannot comprehend, none of us can do a thing about it, except to honor a loved one in some grand gesture later.

Wanting to raise money for lung cancer research, Mark's son Rob Belanger and a close friend Chris Federico had developed the Belanger Federico Foundation in honor of Mark, and Chris' mom, Susannah, who also had died of cancer. Enter idea genius Sharon Perfetti, who, with Federico, proposed forming an offshoot of the foundation, and Cool Kids Campaign was born. This fantastic Baltimore- based nonprofit organization offers a series of unique programming for kids with cancer as they muddle through this horrid, life-altering disease that entails chemotherapy, radiation, countless hospital visits, and painful procedures.

Sharon serves as Cool Kids Campaign's executive director, Chris as president, and Rob its chairman. A fourth co-founder is Baltimorean Kimmie Meissner, World and U.S. champion figure skater. (Belanger Federico Foundation was eventually dissolved.) Along with Ken on the board of advisors are these sports-related names: Brooks Robinson, Steve Rogers, Bruce Laird, Scott McGregor and Johnny Holliday.

Ten successful years later, Cool Kids Campaign is national and solidly supported by corporate and private donations. It thrives with a cool list of

FREE programs to assist kids with cancer – and their families – such as one-on-one tutoring in the Cool Kids Learning Center, care packages, a teen club, siblings support group, preschool play sessions, free social activities and much more.

"Hospitals like Johns Hopkins and Children's National Medical Center are great at research and treatments and have wonderful Child Life Programs," said Steve Stuck, father of the late MacKenzie Stuck, one of the original 'cool kids.' "But when a child is discharged, a family naturally wants to get the heck out of there. Then what? The child is normally immune-suppressed and cannot attend school. Even trying to 'get away' as a family is extremely challenging because it's necessary to stay nearby 'just in case.' That's where Cool Kids Campaign comes in – focused on quality-of-life programs, learning opportunities and social activities with other kids and families going through similar life-altering experiences."

Rob Belanger thinks his father Mark "would have been ecstatic about the campaign if he were alive. Dad went out of his way to bring smiles to kids' faces when he signed autographs. He would probably have become an ambassador to help the program along and rally with his time and energy. I can hear him saying to his teammates, 'C'mon! We're going to pump this thing up! Let's raise money!' He'd be completely in their faces. I think he would have really loved the organization and what we are accomplishing."

"The Cool Kids Campaign philosophy is that kids are kids, regardless if they are sick or healthy," Perfetti said. "Every kid wants to feel cool even if they don't feel well. As we decide how to help these kids and best use the donated dollars, we try to make them forget, at least for a little while, that they are fighting for their lives."

"Cancer kids have a hard enough life," Stuck said. "It's wonderful to be able to have fun with other kids 'just like them.' Therein lies the genius of the Cool Kids Learning Center – a place to stay academically and socially engaged with other kids and people who understand what they're going though."

Learn more about Cool Kids Campaign and how you can help: coolkidscampaign.org.

Life needs diversions – like baseball

You know that reflective, somber mood that can overtake us after attending a funeral? I was in that mood when I wrote this.

I don't much prefer to attend funerals – who does? Yet I do like to write when my mind is swirling in such a pensive frame of mind. On the afternoon that I wrote this, the plan was to return from a funeral Mass of a former coworker – "Marvelous Melba" I called her – and write a *Mrs. Singy* column about baseball clothing.

But the topic of baseball in any shape or form on a gloomy and cloudy funeral day seemed totally inconsequential. Who cares about anything baseball when we feel sad? Can't take that to heaven.

In many conversations with Ken, he explains that sports are a release – a diversion. Pure entertainment. Maybe that's why we need activities like watching baseball – so as not to walk around like post-funeral zombies 24/7, contemplating the woe of the world.

Maybe without stimulating playoffs and energizing championship games on which to focus, a depressed fan wouldn't have been able to get out of bed in the morning. Maybe without the release of cheering and the cohesiveness of fans, some people would be lying on the floor at home inconsolable and heartbroken after something tragic had happened in their lives. Maybe they needed the diversion to take their minds off of a dilemma; a small reason to get dressed and put one foot in front of the other to go watch a sport they heartily adore. They stand up to clap, cheer, holler, and smile their way through a baseball game because it makes them feel better.

Maybe for some of you, baseball (or another favorite sport) has helped to get you through? Divorce, job loss, house repossession, traffic accident, or, God forbid, a family tragedy. Or even just an overall rotten day.

Yes, life needs diversions, like sports. We crave trivial day-to-day activities to balance the heavy. We need distractions so that we are able to slip out of somber moods … and once again think happy thoughts. For many, baseball equals happy.

Clothed in baseball

Since I write solo in my Baltimore home office without an editor, I often ask a fellow writer and friend, Nancy Menefee Jackson (who edited this book), to review my stories before I submit them for publication.

So when Nancy read a story titled *Clothed in baseball*, which I had written for my former YESnetwork.com blog, she admitted she didn't like it – the story was weak.

Nancy knows.

The idea had evolved during a week when one Mrs. Singy was a tad "dry" for a topic. So instead I tackled the laundry. (Thrilling. Proof of writer's block.) After padding barefooted around the house putting away clean clothes predominantly stamped with the *NY* logo, I wrote about how us Singletons could open a New York Yankees store with all the baseball-related clothes we own.

The piece rambled on like this: *... hats, socks, sweatshirts, knit caps, windbreakers, workout clothes, basketball shorts, winter coats, robes and T-shirts – oh so many T-shirts! Long-sleeved, short-sleeved, no sleeves. There's even a pair of NYY underwear at the bottom of the laundry basket (whom they belong to, I'll never tell). The kitchen drawer holds a neatly folded NY Yankees pinstriped apron (which Ken should wear when he grills to avoid barbeque sauce splattering on his favorite YES T-shirt). Our shirts are screened with "Property of YES NETWORK" ... "Why New York is better than New York: We never traded Nolan Ryan" ... "My Yankees Baseball" ... "YES HD" ... and various players' names and numbers white-on-navy across the backs.*

I continued the boring clothing chronicle about how these New York-based garments have long since replaced logos of other baseball positions that Ken has held: shirts and jackets boasting MSG Network, FOX Sports, Montreal Expos and The Sports Network in Canada. And way before those, we once wore a series of orange and black Baltimore Orioles items.

When Nancy suggested spicing up the subject by maybe tying the T-shirts to memories, still – I had nothing. After all, Ken constantly brings home baseball stuff, so there isn't much nostalgia there; we have lived and breathed the sport for several decades. (*Baseball Is Life* is the most significant T-shirt in our house.)

No, there wasn't even much to reminisce about that pair of NYY underwear, other than they were purchased in a Cooperstown, N.Y., gift shop during a pleasant family trip to Induction Weekend. (Ok, they're mine, alright?)

Enough about baseball clothes. (Nancy warned you it was weak).

Then I read a comment posted under the *Mrs. Singy* column from a Yankee fan that knew how to attach true feeling to a New York Yankees garment, putting my dim words to shame with a feeble story about NY clothing.

This fan's anecdote was about how Yankees baseball pulled him through cancer. "It was like being in a safe environment for a few hours," he wrote. "One that made me forget, even for the shortest of times, that I was sick or in pain."

When this fan lost his hair during three rounds of chemo, he purchased a new NY cap that he will "never get rid of," he said. "It's worn heavily, but I can't discard a cap that did so much for me."

He said he feels the same way about the entire Yankees franchise – a team that helped him greatly through a tough time, providing a distraction from ill health. Luckily, he was in remission.

Now my collection of colorful NYY caps has meaning. As I donned the canary-yellow one to wear while walking the dog, I recalled this fan's bittersweet story – how a simple item like a baseball cap can evolve into such sweet significance for an ordinary baseball fan.

Blind baseball passion

At a Yankees/Orioles baseball game, a small group of blind fans filed into the row in front of us.

What must that be like, to attend a baseball game as a blind person? For someone to experience what is usually a visual sport yet be able to hear only its sounds. The distinct crack of a wooden bat, the hearty *"BOO!"* of an enormous crowd, and the silky voice of a PA announcer.

Visually much would be missed, such as the active images on a stadium's giant screen and spotless white uniforms before they're muddied up. And we've all watched the drunken disorderly fan being escorted by security out of the stadium.

They say blind people are greatly attuned to the other four senses. What we may take for granted, they may envelope in its entirety: the meaty aroma of a hot dog, the salty flavor of a soft pretzel, or groping their way along hard plastic stadium seats.

Two of the blind fans at that game were a young couple sharing an earpiece while they listened to the action on the radio. Their heads remained cheek-to-cheek for almost all of the nine innings.

Endearing.

The group of blind people knew when to cheer for a good play or a home run. It didn't seem to matter to them which of their senses led the open-air experience, only that their passion for baseball led them to the game.

Meeting Mrs. Kitty Kaat

I didn't meet MaryAnn Kaat until after she died. Somehow we were never at Yankee Stadium simultaneously during any games that Ken announced with Jim "Kitty" Kaat on YES Network. (Jim is a former MLB pitcher and Gold Glove winner for 16 seasons; his career spanned 25 years.)

When Kitty and his family had organized a memorial party for MaryAnn, it was then I learned all about the wife Jim was completely in love with, as he voiced a stirring tribute about her. By far, the event was the most moving memorial I had ever attended – not a memorial service, but a party! (Everyone should leave the earth that way; it was absolutely magnificent.)

Picture an enormous white tent pitched on the waterfront lawn of the Kaats' residence on the east coast of Florida; round tables covered in white linen; a long buffet of scrumptious food edging the tent; and one hundred of the Kaats' friends and family from around the country, gathered on a clear butter-yellow sunny day.

In the covered walkway leading to the front door, Kitty had hung large beautiful photographs of him and MaryAnn in various stages of their marriage. At the party, he wore the same Hawaiian shirt and white pants that he wore when they were married.

At one point during Jim's homage describing his effervescent Italian wife, a boat motored by and tooted its horn. For those of us who believe in signs, it seemed as if MaryAnn was saying, "Thanks – I'm watching all of this!"

Later, guests had the option of writing messages with black markers on environmentally friendly helium balloons and releasing them. I wrote, *"MaryAnn, we would have been friends ... happy heaven*" and let the balloon slither out of my hands toward the bright blue sky, wishing I had had the chance to befriend her.

Their home's decor symbolized her colorful personality as an upbeat and energetic gal. Jim had invited his guests to wander through the house at whim to read the plethora of plaques, photos, inspirational quotes, book titles and entertaining artwork scattered amidst multi-colorful furniture. What a wonderful collection of whimsical items.

It was a splendid yellow *HAPPY HOUSE*. A quote on a wooden rooster plaque in the kitchen read: *Life is always in progress*. Indeed, life was in full motion that day as MaryAnn's friends and family honored her blessed life.

In the living room was a notebook of a collection of hundreds of poems Kitty had written to his wife daily; some supporting MaryAnn through her illness. That day, I had encouraged Jim to publish them, and he ran with the idea.

Some months later in the mail, I received his new book of poetry: *Dance of Love; Dance of Life: Poetry by Jim Kaat,* attributed to his wife and titled after a sculpture in their backyard. In the book's Acknowledgments, Jim wrote: "I wish to acknowledge Suzanne Singleton, the wife of Ken Singleton, my 10-year TV partner while covering the New York Yankees. Suzanne encouraged me to produce this book after attending a memorial celebration for MaryAnn. At the service I recited the final poem I wrote to the love of my life the day before she died. Suzanne saw there were many more and thought they would be worthy of a book."

Behind that garden sculpture now is a memory garden that includes a plaque with MaryAnn's name, the extraordinary woman who etched Kitty's heart for 22 years … *MaryAnn Montanaro Kaat.*

Dance of Love, Dance of Life
Poetry by a self proclaimed dumb jock

When I opened the lumpy envelope containing Jim Kaat's just-published poetry book, *Dance of Love; Dance of Life: Poetry by Jim Kaat*, one word came to mind – SENSATIONAL. Every person after they die should be honored with such an exquisite tribute.

For several reasons I was "wowed." For one: who would expect a self-proclaimed "dumb jock" to go so deep? And I don't mean to left field. And two:

the contents of Jim's book depicts a love so sturdy and affectionate between husband and wife, even if we didn't know Kitty, we would have shed a tear for the tenderness he offered, and for the sadness and helplessness he experienced watching his beloved bride of 22 years wither away with cancer.

The couple's love shall endure forever, printed in a tomato-red hardback book. MaryAnn's bright face bursts from almost every page as the reader watches her live, hug, swim, laugh, kiss, share, sit and love Jim Kaat right back "mutually," as she once told him. And if Kitty's poems aren't beautiful enough, two surprises are included in the poetry collection: eight of MaryAnn's family members and friends wrote their loving thoughts. And, there are several pages of MaryAnn's notes to Jim in her handwriting. What a charming testimony of marriage.

"Facing Mickey Mantle with the bases loaded was relatively easy," wrote Jim in *Dance of Love*, as he anguished over how he would pen his last words to his wife. He recited this to MaryAnn on the day before she took her last breath in July 2008:

Farewell my beautiful queen
The most magnificent woman I've met or seen

I look forward to seeing you again some day
I'll recognize you as soon as I see you

You'll be the one that stands out from the crowd
The dynamic outspoken one, free-spirited Italian
Maybe a bit boisterous and loud

You'll always be with me in spirit, my guiding light
Even though you're gone from my sight

Proud to be baseball lovin' Americans

There is nothing more all-American than baseball. Unless you count watching baseball in Washington, D.C., a city where an American can feel enormously proud to be a United States citizen. For all that the town symbolizes ... for all it holds ... for what it is ... the District of Columbia provides us with a mecca of red, white and blue emotion.

Following Ken into D.C. for the Yankees/Nationals series one June, we bee-bopped around D.C. on the Yankees day off to walk around the memorials, monuments and plethora of fluttering American flags … Lincoln Memorial, Washington Monument, The White House and war memorials.

There sit splendid and touching tributes to our country's history, to our fellow citizens and war heroes, to past presidents – right in Baltimore's back yard only an hour south – and rarely have we taken the time to visit, appreciate and honor that.

It was at the Vietnam War Memorial wall where I felt more emotional. The hundreds upon hundreds – make that tens of thousands (over 58,000) of soldiers' names etched into that sad gray granite wall brought on silent tears. Each person had died for our country. For us. For America's freedom.

As I stopped to read some of the names, I thought about their families who have had to continue life without their sons and daughters, brothers and sisters, fathers and mothers, uncles and aunts, husbands and wives, and friends. I thought about the day these families had received the dreaded news – maybe in the form of unannounced uniformed military personnel appearing at their front doors, or in the way of a special delivery telegram – a day that altered their lives and hearts forever.

Al Bumbry, Ken's former Oriole teammate and best friend, served in Vietnam. He once told Ken that the platoon leader was the one responsible for writing letters to families after a fellow soldier died. Luckily, Bumbry didn't have to write any such letter. He said he was extremely careful as a platoon leader, not only because he cared deeply about his fellow soldiers, but because he wanted to get back and play baseball.

Visiting the wall caused recall of the platinum P.O.W. bracelet I have had sitting in my jewelry box for four decades, etched with the name LT. COL.

SHELDON BURNETT. I was a 12-year-old girl in the 1970s when my hippie cousin Jeanie had ordered a bracelet for me and my older brother and sister. I may not have understood then all that the Vietnam War stood for, but I knew that Lt. Col. Burnett was a real person in a real family. I wore that bracelet for many years.

As I wrote this, I searched on the Internet for the Vietnam Veterans Memorial and found my soldier. I learned that his remains were discovered in 2004. After all that time, what must it have been like for the family to learn that news? Since the 1970s, through what hell had they journeyed not knowing, without closure?

Thank you, Lt. Col. Sheldon Burnett. And every other soldier. Thank you for serving America.

Seems fitting that I had written this piece and soon after listened to these words sung by a guitarist in Baltimore's Inner Harbor as tall ships from other countries were visiting. Sing with me …

And I'm proud to be an American
Where at least I know I'm free

And I won't forget the men who died
Who gave that right to me

And I gladly STAND UP next to you
And defend her still today

Cuz there ain't no doubt I love this land
God bless the U.S.A.

(lyrics by Lee Greenwood)

There will be no crying over the start of the season

One would think in the many years of facing the start of another eight-month baseball season, a wife might become accustomed to the idea of a baseball husband going on the road. Not so.

Every year I feel weepy on the day Ken first leaves on a plane to Tampa, Fla., to catch up with the New York Yankees for spring training. There he attends production meetings, receives his media credentials, collects press guides, announces TV games and hits a few buckets of golf balls while warm weather is in favor.

Here we go again … it's baseball season.

One year as I cried over making raisin toast, our then 12-year-old daughter asked, "What's wrong, Mom?" I had awoken with a half-empty bed occupied several hours earlier by Ken's warm 6-foot-4 body (can you hear the violin?). He had kissed my cheek at 5:30 a.m. before departing for the airport.

"Nothing," I said, sniffling. She stared at me as I stirred my coffee. "Okay," I answered, "I don't like when Daddy leaves. I miss him already."

I stopped crying lest I got her tears started; she had school on which to focus. So we moved along with our day: drove the kids to school; had a quick coffee chat with a friend; stopped at the gym; and then back to my home office to write.

Then Ken's first road trip came about; that year was the New York Yankees' new stadium opening, and we were fortunate to be able to join him in those festivities and a few days walking around the city. Ken stayed another week in New York as the kids and I trained home to honor their school schedule.

Maybe the tears went deeper. They may have been also for the fact that when the kids were younger, we accompanied Ken to spring training and lived in Florida for a month. I'm a writer – I can work from anywhere. That was during Ken's days on radio with the Montreal Expos. They gave him a housing stipend which we used to rent beautiful new houses in West Palm Beach near golf courses and beaches – particularly welcoming when northerly winds were howling in Maryland and we could leave behind the gloves, coats, scarves and boots.

No matter how glamorous people believe Ken's job is, the reality is that his schedule is challenging for family life. His absence creates one less plate on the dinner table and one less person in our house as we miss him, and he misses much family life.

The death of the offseason takes a slight adjustment on all of our parts: Ken, me, the kids. I might add that he is a functional 'house husband' in the offseason. Now who's gonna grocery shop, make the beds and cook spaghetti while I write?

No wonder I'm crying.

Mr. & Mrs. Singy in Nicaragua 2015 for Dennis Martinez's charity golf tournament (Singleton photo)

"If I didn't make it in baseball,
I won't have made it working.
I didn't like to work."

– Yogi Berra 1925 – 2015

6th INNING

Yankee Panky

Singleton grateful to Steinbrenner

When George Steinbrenner died in 2010, I could imagine how the corporate phones were ringing off the hooks in the New York Yankees office because at home in Baltimore, our landline and Ken's cell never stopped jingling.

Radio stations that typically phone Ken during the baseball season for interviews about the game in general double their calls when big news breaks. That week they wanted Ken's reaction and thoughts on Steinbrenner.

My husband felt sad and melancholy when he heard the news. He happened to be golfing during the All-Star break; because his cell phone sounded repeatedly on the links, he stopped after nine holes to drive home, handle the incoming interviews and quietly process the news.

Yankees fans everywhere grieved, along with the Steinbrenner family.

"Mr. Steinbrenner was always good to me," said Ken back then. "This is not a good week for the Yankees and their fans. We had just learned about [longtime P.A. announcer] Bob Sheppard's death a few days before."

Twenty years ago, Steinbrenner had the final say whether to hire Ken as a television broadcaster. In Steinbrenner's Tampa office before spring training at Legends Field, Ken and two MSG (Madison Square Garden) executives met with the Yankees owner.

"I don't think our fans are going to like you," Ken recalled Mr. Steinbrenner's comment.

"How come?" asked Ken.

"I can recall all the bad things you used to do to us," said Mr. Steinbrenner about Ken as a Baltimore Orioles right-fielder and designated hitter.

"With all due respect, Mr. Steinbrenner," Ken responded. "I was just doing my job." To which he replied, "Well, you did it very well."

After Ken left Tampa, he was unsure he would be offered a seat in the booth to broadcast for the Yankees. Yet the next day he received an affirmative phone call.

"I appreciate the opportunity – and every single minute I've been there," Ken said. "Mr. Steinbrenner said I could work for his team even though I never played for the Yankees … probably because I am from New York."

Ken feels grateful that even after YES Network was established 15 years ago, Steinbrenner kept him around. Over the years he hasn't encountered the boss often because Steinbrenner was usually in Tampa.

"I guess he liked what he saw on TV," said Ken. "If he had had a problem with our broadcasts, I'm sure we would have heard."

About Mr. Steinbrenner as a team owner, he said, "I have a lot of respect for the way he built the Yankees into a championship franchise. When he bought the team in 1973 they weren't very good."

I would venture to guess that the eight All-Star Yankees that year played their hearts out during the All Star game, in honor of an all-star owner. It was suitable that his team was well represented (with more players than any other that game) and fitting that Steinbrenner chose All Star game day to find his way to heaven.

__Ken__ in TV action for YES Network with __Joe Girardi__ before Joe became the NY Yankees' manager. "I appreciate the opportunity – and every single minute I've been there," Ken said of the job he loves.

Hot doggin' with a Yankee's mom, Margy Teixeira

Funny when our friends ask where our seats are when the kids and I attend a baseball game in New York or Baltimore, thinking for some crazy reason we're "in the suites." No. Baseball families sit in the stadium sections, too; we are mere fans capable of fetching hot dogs and Cracker Jack like everyone else.

So around the fourth inning at a Yankees' home opener in 2009, I craved some nice healthy chicken fingers; my then-12-year-old daughter felt an onion ring urge. (You're supposed to eat this junk – it's a baseball game.) In line, we bumped into Margy Teixeira, mother of New York Yankees first baseman Mark Teixeira, and his sister Elizabeth. In Baltimore as a staff writer for *The Catholic Review* newspaper, I had interviewed Margy Teixeira and her husband John "Tex" Teixeira; she and I had hit it off immediately, being that we are Italian. Nice friendly people were those Teixeiras. That's Baltimore for ya, hon.

At Yankee Stadium, Margy was on the quest for eight hot dogs and eight water bottles for her crew – who, it turns out – had to wait a while to munch because we stood in line for an hour and 15 minutes. Seems there was a french fry shortage for starters; plus we had picked the slowest line. (Perhaps the food service employees had a few kinks to untangle on their first day in the new Yankee Stadium?)

We hardly noticed how long we waited or that we missed several innings, because Margy and I chattered nonstop. She noticed too late – oops – that she had missed one of Mark's at-bats as Ken and his broadcast partner, Michael Kay, announced plays on the TV screen above the concession stand. All in the name of a tasty hot dog.

Although we had become a tad squirmy after an hour, feeding our stomachs certainly was *not* more important than the frazzled girl trying to keep up with hungry and irritated fans wishing instead they had stayed in their seats and waved down a hot dog vendor. By the time we stepped up to the cashier, she looked at me forlornly with furrowed eyebrows and asked desperately, "What inning is it?"

I felt sorry for her, the pitiful darling. I'm fairly certain it wasn't the game in which she was interested – she desired the *end* of the game, and the conclusion of the perpetual line.

Margy and I finally received our orders, not entirely accurate, but why sweat the small stuff. Somehow the price of one of my items ended up on her bill. I insisted on paying her back but she waved away the offer.

Thanks for the onion rings, Margy! You'll definitely be missed around Yankee Stadium.

*At Yankee Stadium, Baltimoreans **Elizabeth Teixeria** (left) with her mom **Margy Teixeria** rooting on brother and son, **Mark Teixeria**, NY Yankees first baseman. Margy died in December 2015. (Singleton photo)*

Always Yankees connected (even in Italy)

Waiting for a flight to Boston out of Baltimore one summer, a Mark Teixeira-jerseyed guy approached Ken and I in the airport restaurant to meet and greet.

His name was Mike and he was headed on his honeymoon from Auburn, N.Y., along with his new bride Erin with a bridal corsage pinned to her shirt. The lovebirds asked for an autograph and photo of Ken, which I snapped of the three of them. They went merrily on their way after sending us a complimentary beverage in appreciation.

Always Yankees connected.

In October 2007 in Venice, Italy, Ken and I stumbled across a kiosk of NYY caps of various colors: pink, red and white. NYY caps in Italy? Why not? Yankee fans travel, too … they're everywhere! A few recognized Ken in Venice as we walked along twisted alleys and crossed miniature bridges.

"Ken Singleton, what are you doing here?" one fan called out. With his standard answer to that question, Ken smiled and said, "Everyone has to be somewhere."

Always Yankees connected.

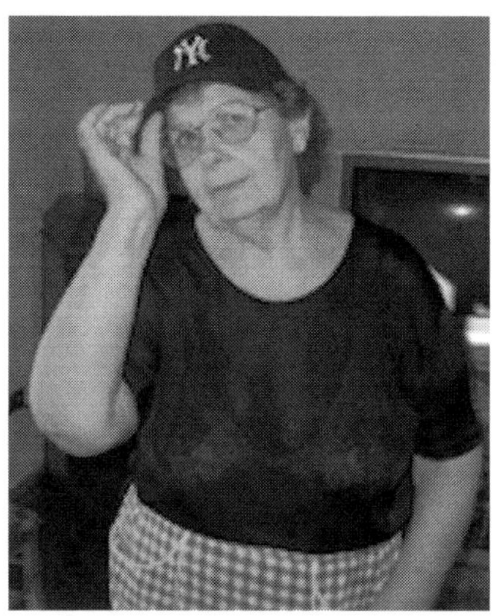

*Suzanne's cousin **Tina Mossa** in Luras, Sardinia, Italy, shows off her Yankee cap (before she cooked a wonderful meal!). The Singletons carted over to Italy a box of Yankee merchandise to dole out to cousins on a 2007 visit to Mrs. Singy's grandparents' village. (Singleton photo)*

And if there weren't Yankee fans in Italy before we got there, we created some. Thanks to the kindness of Connie Schwab in NYY's Media Relations (who had provided a large box of merchandise to take along to my cousins in Sardinia, Italy), Ken and I doled out baseball caps, pens and key chains, leaving the NY logo mark around the ancient village of Luras, my grandparents' *paesa*.

Always thinking Yankees.

Riding home from Pennsylvania after a family birthday celebration, Ken turned on the radio and the voices of Suzyn Waldman and John Sterling erupted loudly and clearly from station 880 AM … all the way to Baltimore.

Always Yankees connected.

When that signal turned to static, Ken flipped open his iPhone, touch-screened a few buttons, and *ta-da* … YES Network sounded over the Internet. Had we been home, the Yankees would have been making plays right in our living room on that impeccable hi-def image which shows every whisker on a player's face.

Had Ken not been home, we can still watch him announcing games – the beauty of a DirectTV baseball package.

Always Yankees connected.

Michael Kay's wedding, so Hollywood

New York City. The Plaza Hotel. Across from the northwest corner of Central Park. Black tie attire. Two New York personalities tie the knot. Room full of baseball celebrities and pros. Yankees and YES Network bosses. Officiated by former mayor of New York. Beautiful people in gowns and tuxedos. Were we on a movie set???

Of all the swanky details to impress a person at the lavish Michael Kay and Jodi Applegate wedding Feb. 12, 2011, the one that pinned this Italian girl to her seat was eyeing *THE Johnny Cammareri* – a character in my all-time favorite, seen-it-a-hundred-times movie, *Moonstruck*, played by Danny Aiello. Only if Cher had walked into The Plaza would I have been more keyed up.

We've known Michael since Ken began announcing Yankees games on YES Network, yet we never knew Aiello was his uncle. *It's Johnny! Johnny Cammareri!* (Apparently, Michael never knew *Moonstruck* was my favorite movie, or he may have shared that little tidbit.)

*Actor **Danny Aiello** singing to his nephew, the groom **Michael Kay** and bride **Jodi Applegate** at their wedding in New York City 2011. Michael is one of Ken's broadcast partners on YES Network. (Singleton photo)*

The movie is timeless. For *Moonstruck* aficionados, *you* get it. Say it with me:

"Johnny – Ronnie's brother"

[Loretta] "You got a hat? Use your hat."
[Johnny] "Ok, I got my hat, all right.

[Cosmo] "You'll have your eyes opened for you, my friend.
[Johnny] I have my eyes open.

[Johnny] "In time you will see that this is the best thing."

[Loretta] "In time you'll drop dead and I'll come to your funeral in a red dress!"

In Baltimore, where I am director of the Promotion Center for Little Italy, *Moonstruck* is the first film shown in our summer Little Italy Open Air Film Fest. Dozens of times I've watched this film over the years, finally trading in a worn-out VHS version for a DVD. (Though no one much enjoys watching it with me since I quote most of the lines - can't help myself.)

Oh, please excuse me. Here I am gushing over *Moonstruck* and *Johnny*. Back to the wedding – impressive in itself. Absolutely superb. A Hollywood-type-picture-perfect ceremony and reception. Jodi was stunning in her strapless white gown (which she did *not* change three times, contrary to the blundered reports in *The New York Post*). Michael looked very handsome sweating in his tuxedo.

As New York celebrities, Michael and Jodi know many people – the grand ballroom had not a spare inch in which to shake our booties to the tunes of a fabulous 14-member band. The Kays also have a sense of humor. Who would have expected such a posh venue to serve pizza, hotdogs, wings and sliders during cocktail hour? There was also a sushi bar and other lavish appetizer fare.

We were served a fabulous white-gloved sit-down dinner and upon exiting the event well after midnight, a table of clear jars boasting a variety of candy bars were there for the taking. Very fun.

Yes, the wedding was indeed a magnificent event with several very distinctive details, like "Johnny Cammareri" singing to the bride and groom on the dance floor.

We could have been on a movie set after all.

Ken Singleton *and* ***Michael Kay****, friends and fellow TV broadcasters on YES Network, at Michael's wedding 2011. (Singleton photo)*

I pledge allegiance to my lime green Yankees jacket

New York Yankees merchandise doesn't consist of only blue and white pinstripes, as merchandise shopping fans know. Some creative genius along the design line had fun with color – maybe to appeal to the ladies – and produced hats, T-shirts and jackets of all hues.

My hat rack holds NYY caps in lime green, shocking pink, pastel pink, sunlight yellow and really red, plus, of course, the traditional dark blue. Ken once gifted me for Christmas a lime green Yankees jacket. In the winter, I wear it to the gym or to power walk the neighborhood (and you can bet the neighbors see me coming – no reflectors needed.)

Yet comments about the vivid color aren't the only ones flung my way. Because I'm a native Baltimore girl wearing a New York team's logo (and worse, a rivalry of the Orioles), freedom of speech comes into play as friends have their say about my precious Yankees merchandise.

Mrs. Singy *in her beloved lime green Yankees jacket and cap. (Singleton photo)*

"Take off that jacket while you're around me" or "I'd like to burn that T-shirt." We listen to these and other wise-guy remarks, me and the kids. Someone might say that my son's NYY cap is hurting his eyes or making him gag. Funny friends, aren't they? My standard reply is, "The Yankees feed our kids and pay for tuition" (and buy me pretty shoes, but I leave out that part).

It's a bit of a quandary, being that I was once a big Orioles fan. But akin to baseball players being traded team to team, the kids and I switched our team allegiance after Ken began to call Yankee games on MSG Network over twenty years ago before YES Network was created.

Actually, we've discovered it's not too tough being Yankees fans – it's rather fun. We love riding the train from Baltimore to New York City, and it's quite exciting to watch the team make it to the World Series so often. We love the enthusiasm in the stands, and … Yankee fans are everywhere!

At first I thought we could be fans of both the Yankees and the Orioles, yet when the O's hosted the Yankees, we were traumatized … which team should we root for? Whose T-shirt should we wear? The first few seasons after Ken began announcing Yankees games, I sat in the stands in street clothes and rooted for no one. That felt odd.

And if you think his wife gets teased, you should hear Baltimoreans comment to Ken about announcing for the Yankees. Poor hubby. O's fans think he should have black and orange running through his veins. Of course, he will be an Oriole forever, and extremely proud of his 10 years on the team and his World Series ring. Yet his career is with the Yankees and he enjoys it immensely. (Side trivia: Ken was born in Manhattan and grew up in Mount Vernon, N.Y. The Singletons lived in a house once owned by a former Brooklyn Dodger, Ralph Branca.)

Let Baltimore fans tease us all they want, we're wearing our Yankees merchandise and that's that. And I will continue to pledge allegiance to my lime green Yankees jacket. That is, until Ken brings home a different color.

***Mrs. Singy** and then 8-year-old "**Little Singy**" wait for Ken in the New York Yankees lobby after a 2005 game. (Singleton photo)*

***Ken** in the YES Network booth with two of his broadcast partners, **Michael Kay,** and retired NY Yankee **Paul O'Neill**. Other YES TV personalities who also played for the Yankees include **John Flaherty, David Cone** and **Al Leiter.** Ken loves working with each of them. (Singleton photo)*

*The youngest Singy as a pre-teen in the dugout with **Alex Rodriguez** in 2007. (Singleton photo)*

*Former NY Yankee **Bernie Williams** and the **Singletons** in Longboat Key, Fla., after Bernie's jazz concert on the beach. (Singleton photo)*

7TH INNING

Game Gab

Let's talk spit

Spit is gross. Thankfully, I am not a spitter, not now nor as a softball player. I didn't like it in elementary school when the Catholic schoolboys made spitballs, nor do I like seeing a stranger hock a loogie. (I am gagging at this very topic.)

So the age-old question from us spit-haters is WHY? Why do baseball players spit?

Camels and alpacas spit. So do cobras. Babies spit up. But baseball players are none of those (some might argue).

Basketball players don't spit. Ice hockey players don't spit. We don't notice pro golfers spitting on the links. Football players might spit some, but since they have to lie on the turf after tackling each other, they might be more careful about where their saliva lands.

Spit is an appropriate word for a vulgar action and an absolute nasty habit. Socially, spitting on someone is one of the rudest and most disrespectful things you can do to another human; spitting is considered taboo in some parts of the world.

Ken says it's out of nervous energy that baseball players spit. Some are spitting not saliva, but tobacco juice and sunflower seeds. Although he says he spits, I have not seen Ken spit (he must have as a player). By the way, Ken prefers the word *expectorate*.

Call it what you will – spittle, saliva, spit – I have to agree with John Payne from Simsbury, Conn., who wrote Ken a four-page letter about spitting. Yes, FOUR pages, on pretty blue stationery. His opinion was quite entertaining.

"There is too much spitting by all the players on all the teams," wrote Mr. Payne. (He was quite serious about the topic, too – he typed in ALL CAPS.) "I wonder if these players spit on the floor at home or in restaurants? Do they do all this spitting when they go out with their wives or girlfriends?"

He thinks the Yankees superstars are the ones who spit the most. So I ran into the TV room to see for myself and to get Ken's spit input as he watched a Yankees / A's game. He suggested I count the number of times the players spit in an inning. Three spits later, I was outta there.

I couldn't watch it any more than Mr. Payne, who said he is so offended by the ongoing spitting that he makes sure to eat dinner before he watches a baseball game on television. It is hard for him to finish his meal while observing "this nasty, unsightly, unsanitary and unhealthy practice."

He would like Ken and the other announcers to discuss this spitting problem with the camera people so they don't show any spitting on air.

Ken said that's a bit tricky. How are they supposed to know when someone is ready to spit? True.

There's only one other solution then, according to Mr. Payne. He would like to request of the baseball commissioner to make a ruling against spitting during games. "Make an agreement," he suggested, "to help solve this disgusting practice."

I'm with you on that one, Mr. Payne. Maybe this is the reason it's so challenging for me to sit through nine innings. (Can I blame it on the spitting?)

The fan wrote that he has seen "players spit on their hands, rub the baseball, rub dirt on their hands, then put their hand back in their mouth. This cannot be very sanitary or healthy. My relatives, my friends and I … would love to be able to eat and enjoy our meal while we watch the Yankees on YES Network."

I'm guessing Mr. Payne would be very upset if spitballs were still legal.

A stat I'd like to know: More NY logos or Mickey Mouse ears?

For those of you who have had the magical delight of visiting Disney World, you are familiar with the zillions of Mickey Mouse ears replicated around the various parks. *Everything* takes on the silhouette of Mickey ears – from the giant roadside water tower nearest Magic Kingdom to the meticulously groomed shrubbery nestled amongst the flawless landscaping … from the fun-to-eat pancakes in the hotel restaurants to the multicolored lollipops in the gift shops.

Mickey ears are *everywhere*.

I figured a repeated logo of such magnitude existed nowhere else … until I stepped into Yankee Stadium. With branding, the Yanks just may have trumped Disney.

A less-than-exciting nine innings during a Friday night Texas vs. New York game propelled me out of my blue stadium seat toward more interesting sights and sounds and into the Yankees store. (Isn't shopping more stimulating than a slow baseball game?)

Having listened to my husband talk baseball for almost 25 years has introduced many a crazy "who cares?" stat which baseball delivers like no other sport. From monumental to trifling, stats are recorded, like the fact that Jarrod Saltalamacchia's name holds the record for the most alphabet letters of any Major Leaguer's name in baseball history … or that the average life of a baseball in the Majors is six pitches. Rubbish like that.

So here's a stat Mrs. Singy would be curious to learn ... how many times is the NY logo replicated throughout Yankee Stadium? Certainly, the number would be unattainable, similar to attempting a count of sand grains on a beach, or the number of times players spit or touch their crotches during a game.

NY logos are *everywhere*. Imprinted on *everything*. From the jumbo photos in the Great Hall to the individual sugar pack sprinkled into my coffee in an attempt to warm up during that 47-degree game.

I'd venture to speculate that no other venue – except maybe Disney World – contains as many logos in one area. Might anyone like to begin counting? It could take a while. Now *that* would make a good stat.

The not-so-all-American game of baseball

Although as a player Ken has experienced three All-Star games (1977, `79, `81), he had the unique opportunity to broadcast the 1998 game in Denver for Major League Baseball International.

I tagged along on the excursion, sucked into the city's energy as it pumped out baseball adrenaline. Every nook and cranny was filled with souvenirs, activities and keyed-up baseball fans in full celebration mode, clearly thrilled to be in such close proximity to their favorite Major Leaguers, and to taste the flavor of Denver.

I met Derek Jeter for the first time during the enormous outside/inside All-Star gala sponsored the previous evening by the Colorado Rockies and Major League Baseball. Quite impressive was that gala (and Derek, who had brought along his sister).

Being the host of an All-Star game gives a city a chance to strut its stuff, so you can envision how many bells and whistles were included that night ... an evening to celebrate Major League Baseball's finest and most popular players and their families, and a chance for the host team to throw the party of the year.

"It's not only about the game," Ken says. "Cities want to put on a good show. They want people to come back."

On game day, working in the booth alongside Gary Thorne (now a Baltimore Orioles play-by-play announcer), Ken's challenge was to deliver the All-Star game to listeners in more than 200 countries around the world, most of whom are not familiar with the sport.

"We had to explain things well," Ken said. "We couldn't take for granted that people knew what we were talking about. When doing regular games, we know that [American] fans are more aware of what's going on."

Emails flowed in during the telecast for Gary and Ken to address as they announced the 69th All-Star Game from Denver's Coors Field.

"We received a lot of questions about strategy," remembers Ken. "Such as, Why does a player sometimes bunt and sometimes not?" The duo would address questions on-air as thoroughly as they could in between plays, to explain the American game to foreigners in New Zealand, Australia, China and other countries around the world.

Ken had the special opportunity to further announce for MLB International, a championship game in 1997 between the Atlanta Braves and the Florida Marlins; the World Series the same year between the Marlins and the Cleveland Indians; and in 1998 the World Series between the Yankees and the San Diego Padres.

Since Minor and Major League players come from far and wide (Argentina, Brazil, Germany, Korea, Netherlands, Italy, South Africa, to name a few) and baseball's popularity continues to grow around the globe, the role of Major League Baseball International (formed in 1989) focuses on worldwide growth of the sport through broadcasting, special events, sponsorship, licensing, etc. Broadcast in 233 countries and territories, Major League Baseball game telecasts are re-transmitted in 17 different languages.

"It was a very rewarding experience," said Ken, "to know that people around the world were enjoying and learning the game."

***Dante Singleton** feeling proud to wear dad's No. 29 jersey. (Singleton photo)*

The Singy kids - growing up in baseball

If I had my way in the bottom of the eighth inning of a baseball game at Yankee Stadium, I'd stay in my seat. Our two younger kids, however, like going upstairs to the press box to see "dad" in live TV action on the YES Network. The TV crew is always welcoming, making room for us in the tight booth and equipping us with water bottles and headsets on which to listen to the broadcast.

*A younger **Dante Singleton** with Ken and former broadcast partner, **Jim "Kitty" Kaat**, in the press box at Yankee Stadium. (below) Then 11-year-old **Angelica Singleton** as "camera operator" in the booth at Oriole Park during a Yankees/Orioles game. (Singleton photos)*

The lights, cameras and action are commonplace for our family since we've been around the scene for years, as we follow Ken around the country. When family or friends are with us, it's refreshing to watch them get fired up experiencing live television up close and meeting other sports celebs in the press box.

It's been amusing over these more than 25 years "talking my way up" to the press level in various baseball stadiums. Seldom was I required to show ID. Seems stadium staff believe a mom with kids in tow is telling the truth claiming she's Mrs. Ken Singleton.

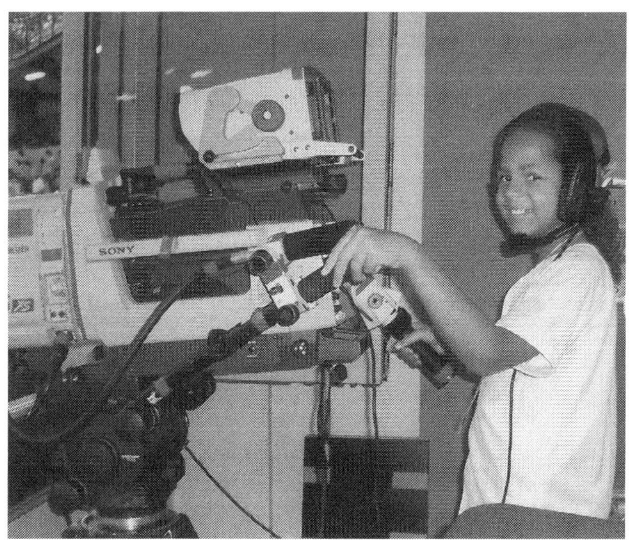

I feel prideful watching hubby work – he's happy around baseball. Turns out, the four kids feel the same way ...

Whereas the two older boys experienced Ken as a player, our two youngest have had the opportunity to watch dad at work in the press box, since he was retired from the Major Leagues before they were born. Today, they are still experiencing behind the baseball scene – and have become avid Yankees fans.

"It's always been pretty surreal to me. He's this public figure that so many people admire, yet he's just my goofy dad," said Dante Singleton, 24. "One night he's at the dinner table, the next night he's on TV. Either way, I'm verbally critiquing his lame jokes. Not everyone can say that about his or her father. It's always cool to be able to see everything behind the scenes, be in the press box, on the production truck, go onto the field before games, meet players and coaches, and watch batting practice from behind the cage. It's the ultimate experience as a baseball fan; words cannot describe how lucky I am."

"People always ask me what it's like to have a famous dad," said Angelica Singleton, 19, and my answer remains the same – it's just like having a regular dad. It's funny to see how he switches to his professional persona when he's at work, since I'm usually around him when he's being a goof at home. I love watching the games on TV when he's announcing – Dante and I always joke, 'How funny would it be if dad made one of his classic, silly jokes on the air?' It was really cool growing up with baseball, and my dad is a big part of why I love the sport. He would always (and still does) update me with scores and stats that I grew to become interested in, and to this day I'm proud to be a passionate fan. I am so grateful to have baseball as such a special part in my life."

The encounters of the two older boys growing up as the kids of a professional baseball player were different than those of their younger brother and sister. Justin and Matt Singleton were on the field, hung out in the dugout during batting practice and, from the stands, watched daddy play ball. They high-fived his friends, to name some: Brooks Robinson, Eddie Murray, Jim Palmer, Doug DeCinces, Rick Dempsey, Rich Dauer, Elrod Hendricks, Gary Roenicke, Dennis Martinez, Tippy Martinez and Cal Ripken Jr.

"I was a little guy, but I remember some of it," said Matt Singleton, 39. "Dad took us into the dugout before games, and we met him in the locker room after the games. I remember being on the field with him and his teammates. I liked watching him hit homeruns and run the bases. We also were allowed to run around the bases after the games with the other players' kids."

"It was great," said Justin Singleton, 36 (age 6 when Ken retired). "To be honest, we didn't appreciate what we were experiencing. Matt and I were too young to realize how cool it was and how fortunate we were to get to run around the clubhouse and play ball with guys like Al Bumbry and Eddie Murray. Like a lot of little boys, I wanted to grow up and be a ball player; I'm sure getting a first-hand look at the big leagues really lit that fire in me, even if I didn't realize it at the time."

Justin's early memories include Orioles Family Day at the ballpark playing a game on the field. He remembers the trainer, the late Ralph Salvon, giving them candy in the clubhouse; and being scared of the Oriole Bird mascot. Matt remembers when the Orioles won the 1983 World Series; and Justin being more afraid of the Bird than he was.

Justin Singleton *as a toddler getting batting instruction from Ken,* ***Benny Ayala*** *(center) and* ***Cal Ripken, Sr.*** *(kneeling).(Singleton photo)*

"He seemed big and intimidating to a kid," said Ken of the mascot. "Then one season beginning, the boys returned and they weren't afraid of him anymore. They started messing with him."

Justin remembers, "Mom getting us cotton candy at the games against dad's wishes. We used to eat it sneakily, in fear that he'd see us from the field." They were only allowed to watch games from behind the home plate net, "so we were protected from foul balls. Although we wanted a chance to catch one." One other memory – which must have been intimidating as well to such a young child – was "dad's car being MOBBED by autograph seekers after games as we tried to leave the ballpark."

*1982 - The Oriole Bird holds **Matt Singleton**, age 6, as Ken looks on. (Singleton photo)*

Wherever Ken has worked – on the field or in the press box – has always made his family proud to stand behind him. "Even now, after he's retired," Matt said, "I like when people are trying to get dad's autograph."

"The best part of it all," said Dante, "is how respected my father is among his peers; his level of professionalism is off the charts. When it's all said and done, I hope I can live to be half the man he is."

SAFE! ***Ken*** *helps son* ***Matthew*** *get on base before* ***Ray Miller,*** *pitching coach, at Memorial Stadium. (Singleton photo)*

*Three generations of baseball enthusiasts at a Phillies game – Ken with 6-year-old grandson and son, **Justin Singleton**. (Singleton photo)*

Anatomy of a broadcaster's briefcase

Fans may be surprised to learn that a baseball broadcaster doesn't show up 15 minutes before a game to go on-air. "That's not the way it works," said Ken, who devotes hours to his baseball homework before picking up a YES Network microphone.

Like the average American, a workday for him is 8-hours-plus, except his is more like second shift – he leaves for the ballpark at 3 p.m. and returns to the hotel around 11:30 (barring extra innings or rain delays).

Let's peek into Ken's 15-pound briefcase, a small black suitcase on wheels, to examine the tools which help him prepare to announce TV games:

1. iPad – Ken visits specific websites daily to check game scores around the leagues and to find out who did what. He learns of players' injuries, special streaks and to see what's happening beyond Yankee Stadium. His preferred sites include:

    - ussportspages.com
    - baseballreference.com
    - playerprofiles.com
    - mlb.com
    - fangraphs.com

2. Press Guides – Ken carries specific ones needed for a particular road trip and of course, the Yankees guide, and keeps each team's press guide in his home office for every American and National League team. He researches historical notes and a plethora of stats. "Press guides tell me everything I want to know about a particular player or team," he said, "even a player's birthday."

3. Scorebook – Designed by his former Montreal Expos radio broadcast partner, Dave Van Horne (veteran broadcaster and current lead play-by-play radio announcer for the Miami Marlins), Ken's scorebook includes room to write notes and track pitchers, game times, team records and next-game pitchers. Ken orders these specially designed scorebooks from a local printer, made thick enough to record an entire season of games.

4. Stats Inc. – Produced each game by Stats Inc., a major informational source for all sports, these notes are waiting in the YES Network booth – a copy for each broadcaster and one for the statistician. “These are very important,” Ken says. “They give good information about that particular game.”

Things he looks for: players on hitting streaks and reaching milestones; injured players and who’s back in the lineup after an injury; what currently makes a team good; why a club is playing better now than at the beginning of the season (or vice versa). “I look for interesting items I think fans may want to know,” Ken said. “What would someone at home ask about this player or team?”

5. Calculator to figure batting averages
6. Legal pads to take notes
7. Honey lemon cough drops to sooth his throat after long games

The first day of a series, or rejoining the Yankees after he’s been off a week, will include the most preparation for Ken. Not every note he collects is used in one game. In a three-game series, for example, he may use some the following day. “It’s better to be over-prepared,” he said, “because you never know when a game is going to go for 15 innings.“

He also prepares a Scouting Report on the starting pitchers – one for each team. “I write three interesting notes about each pitcher and email it to YES’ graphics coordinator, Ryan Rutherford. He’s one of the best.”

After Ken pours over the information he has collected, he is basically ready to announce the game. After settling his belongings into the press box, he visits the clubhouse to chat with players on both teams. Sometimes he peeks into Joe Girardi’s press conference before the game or if he doesn’t have time, he listens to it from the booth. For additional homework, Ken speaks with the visiting team broadcasters; many he knows.

“They see the teams every day,” Ken said. “I don’t. Although I think I know a lot about a team, they have a better insight to help me with the game.”

And if he didn’t spend time preparing? “I would run out of things to talk about,” he said. ”I’d be reacting to the game itself but wouldn’t be able to fill in the blanks. There’s a lot of time in between pitches. I have to fill it with interesting information for the fans.”

Stadium noise is par for the course

On an off day in Spring Training, Ken took time to enjoy one of his favorite pleasures – to watch professional golf at a PGA Tournament in Palm Harbor, Fla., about 30 minutes from Steinbrenner Field.

If you have ever attended a pro golf tournament, you're familiar with how quiet the atmosphere is – a courtesy extended by fans so that golfers can focus and eventually sink miniature white balls into tiny cups in as few strokes as possible.

What amazes Ken is the difference between the hushed atmospheres of a golf tournament versus the deafening one of a baseball stadium.

"Quiet applause is accepted after a shot," Ken said. "Very few fans shout comments, and if they do, it's mostly encouraging. In baseball stadiums, some things that fans yell are not so encouraging and can include disparaging comments about your family members."

In Minnesota on Mother's Day some years back, Oriole Ken was in the on-deck circle warming up when a Twins fan shouted, "It's Mother's Day and even your mother doesn't love you!" Ken went up to bat, hit a home run, and on his way back to the dugout addressed the same guy, "Now even your mother loves me!" That elicited a hearty laugh from the fan's friends.

What people do not realize, Ken said, is that players use the discourteous comments as incentive to play well against the opposing team. "When you're on the road and fans say bad things, you really want to do something to shut them up. Then they might learn to leave you alone."

Ticket takers at pro golf tournaments take more than your entrance fee at the gate – they confiscate all cell phones, too. This is so that phones do not ring during play and people aren't tempted to make calls.

So when it was time for Ken to receive a scheduled phone interview from a Montreal radio station, he was forced to step outside the gates where he could talk Yankees in a comfortable tone of voice without disturbing the quiet on the links (first having to retrieve his cell phone from the front gate staff).

Could you imagine if a Yankee Stadium PA announcer whispered, “Shhh, all quiet please ... Mark Teixeira is up to bat.” Or if a vendor at a golf tournament screamed, “Get your beer here!”

The hype and rowdiness of attending a baseball game is half the fun – no – make that *all* the fun. And who cares if anyone’s yakking on a cell phone? That’s life these days; we can’t hear them anyway over the roar of Yankees fans.

Two different sports, two different atmospheres. The notion supposedly, is that golfers would not be able to concentrate if fans were able to scream at will.

If a pro makes a good putt to take the lead in a tournament, then people get excited. But only after the fact. While a putter is in pendulum motion, no one’s clapping and shouting, “C’mon! Sink the putt, chump!”

I asked Ken what’s the difference with baseball and why doesn’t the noise bother Major Leaguers?

“You just have to concentrate and put all the sounds behind you,” he said. “You can hear the crowd but it’s almost like a buzz in the background because you’re so focused. Even years later, I can remember specific pitches, sequences, what it felt like to hit a baseball and how I swung, all because my concentration was so keen. Not to mention that if you don’t concentrate, you can get hurt while batting or playing the field.”

While comments from fans and the overall racket were challenging to a player, Ken said the noise and excitement is part of the game. “It’s easy to get pumped up in front of 50,000 excited fans.”

Quiet please. Ken is now going to hit golf balls.

Distractions at Tropicana Field

Listen, I try hard to pay attention at Yankees games, honestly I do, but it was odd sitting under a dome at Tropicana Field in Florida versus being in the fresh open air at a ballpark, (although the A/C is a welcome addition during Florida's humidity attacks).

Even when I did settle in to watch the game … ugh. A night of bad plays on the part of the Yankees. As if the roof wasn't enough to keep my eyes roaming away from the field, these did the distraction trick for sure:

- The cowbells … everyone had cowbells! Fans rang them repeatedly to demonstrate their delight when the Rays made a good play or scored. Even the PA system sounded a cowbell! Huh? Is it a Tropicana Field tradition? It's not like the stadium is located in the country with the cows; they're in downtown St. Petersburg. I failed to see the connection.

- A female Rays fan behind us deafeningly shouted almost directly into my left ear *"WOO!!!!!!!! WOO!!!!!!!!"* for nine innings.

- And I couldn't stop staring at a young couple two rows down who seemed to be on a first date. With a phony grin, she constantly nodded to the guy, who talked nonstop about the two teams.

- It was entertaining watching three belligerent drunk girls being escorted out of the stands by security – twice.

- And the guy behind us won first prize for sporting the funniest T-shirt that read: *Boobies Make Me Smile.* (Are you smiling?)

- Then I wondered if it was yet dark outside (that dome again).

- And we were forced to perpetually pay attention to the slew of foul balls coming our way like small white torpedoes (without the bonus of nabbing one ourselves)

- Then there was the creative Cotton Candy caller: "HEY!!!" he screamed frantically, and everyone turned around immediately to look at him. "I got cotton candy," he said quieter and matter-of-factly, with a smirk.

- And how comical to watch the hefty quantities of junk food and beer being shuffled up and down the aisles by vendors and fans, then being consumed by the average gorging American (with my kids asking for money to buy most of it: ice cream, cotton candy, pretzels, soda, french fries).

Yes, a night at a baseball game, try as I may to pay attention, is no easy walk in the ballpark for me. Ken claims I have an attention span issue; that I don't know. Maybe I should just sit in the front row?

What'ya mean, I have to wear high heels to a baseball game?

When Ken and I first dated in 1990 and married the following year, he was a radio color analyst for the Montreal Expos and announced all 180 games. I followed him to Canada and all around the country as he left Baltimore in March and returned at the beginning of October.

As a "newbie" in the baseball wife department, I learned fast that for some reason spouses enjoyed dressing to the nines to attend baseball games: the flashy jewelry, trendy clothes, full makeup, poufy hair and high heels.

What? High heels at a baseball game? I'm just a girl from Baltimore.

Although I was not a player's wife, still the Expos sat me in the family section, which was sectioned off with bright yellow rope like we were special or something. I didn't like it. Fans walked by slowly (everyone knew where the family section was) to stare at us like species in an aquarium, trying to figure out which sparkly fish belonged to which player.

The first season started off informally attired – flat shoes and nice but casual clothes – good enough for a baseball game. Or so I thought. Then I began to feel underdressed sitting with the other wives of players and announcers. We encountered each other before games in the family room, in the stands, and after the games in the tunnel waiting for our husbands to finish work. Although everyone was friendly – it was a nice group of (dressed-up) ladies – there was some eyeing-up for sure. Females are like that.

These were the days of Larry Walker, Delino DeShields, Marquis Grissom, Dennis Martinez, Moises Alou and Gary Carter ... a talented but underpaid team with not much of a fan base – the Expos were lucky to draw 20,000 a game.

As much as I fought the idea of dressing up to sit in a baseball stadium, my younger 30-something self was sucked into the notion of fitting in, so I switched up the look. The flats grew heels, the makeup thickened and additional bling lined the wrists and neck. I transformed into an over-dressed baseball wife who wore skirts, suits and high heels to watch nine innings, hoping no one would accidentally squeeze their hotdog mustard packet too hard in my direction.

Hold everything! What happened to the Dundalk girl who sat in the bleachers at Memorial Stadium on 33rd Street in Baltimore swigging beer with her rowdy friends while rooting for the Orioles and wearing a comfy sweatshirt and sneakers?

Had I really become an overdressed “baseball wife?"

I remember sitting under those fluorescent Olympic Stadium dome lights in Montreal, thinking I couldn't even drink a beer if I wanted one, or pig out on peanuts and blue cotton candy because what would it *look* like? Ack! We were being watched!

Fast forward to today. If I want to swig a beer from a souvenir cup or stuff my face with Bazzini nuts, Carl's steaks or Carvel ice cream at the stadium, I can and I do. Thankfully, there's no yellow-rope seating for our family at Yankees games – we're out of the fish bowl.

And I wear jeans like everyone else. Suits at a baseball game are reserved for the corporate generation who may not have had time to change clothes after work.

Besides, Yankee Stadium is much too big to prance around in high heels.

8th INNING

At Home with the Singys

Ma! You threw away my baseball cards???

Ken wasn't happy when years back Ma Singy tossed his collection of baseball cards from their home in Mount Vernon, N.Y.

"I had a lot of cards," he said, remembering a few stuffed shoeboxes worth. "I used to trade them with my friends." In my late mother-in-law's defense, she didn't remember this when I had asked her about it. She said, "They were probably all bent up and old. I would not throw away anything good."

Being surrounded by baseball cards and other sports memorabilia at the four-day 2010 National Sports Collectors Convention where Ken had been asked to make an appearance reminded my husband of his favored hobby as a kid.

The convention used 350,000-plus square feet of floor space inside the Baltimore Convention Center and attracted upward of 35,000 people. Over 1,000 dealers and exhibitors sold everything from 10-cent baseball cards to a $15,000 Babe Ruth-signed baseball.

"I don't know what cards cost now," Ken said when he returned from his appearance, "but when I was young, we used to buy them for a nickel a pack. They came with bubble gum and five cards. It was really big if you got a Mickey Mantle or a Willie Mays ... but I think purposefully those weren't included in many packs."

For the typical fan, Ken says collecting autographs isn't always about the value of the signed item – that's secondary. The thrill is about having the autograph – especially for kids.

"It's also about the 20 seconds a fan spends with an athlete," Ken said. "They remember that. It's their personal experience." City to city Ken has spotted some of the same die-hard baseball fans waiting in line outside of hotels and ballparks hoping to score a few pros' autographs.

How many times has my husband signed his name in a span of two baseball careers? Like grains of sand on the beach – it would be impossible to count. "I have no clue," he answered, but yes, thousands upon thousands. (It would be an interesting stat to know.)

Does an athlete's hand get tired while signing autographs? You bet. Just think of that Catholic school nun forcing you to write 100 times, "I shall not throw spitballs." Three hours is about tops for Ken's left-handed autographing stamina. He was a switch-hitter, yes, but not with a pen.

When players make appearances, it's common that they sign extra balls for whichever organization contracted them for the autograph session. For instance, at the aforementioned collectors' show, Ken signed six-dozen baseballs in the back room before he even faced an autograph seeker on the Convention Center floor. That was 72 additional "Ken Singletons" to write in his slim, slanty handwriting, on top of the throng of people he signed for who stood in his line between 2:30 and 5:30; he was swamped the entire session.

"I can imagine what it was like on Saturday," Ken said, knowing some of the heavy hitters were in town like Frank "The Big Hurt" Thomas, Eddie Murray, Brooks Robinson, Wade Boggs, Mike Boddicker, the immortal Willie Mays and other Hall of Famers.

The show wasn't only baseball-related. Autograph lines snaked around to end face-to-face with over 70 athletes and entertainment celebrities.

Our then-18-year-old son, Dante, tagged along with dad that Thursday, then returned downtown two days later on his own to get more autographs and meet-and-greet professional wrestlers like Mick Foley, Kurt Angle and Rob Van Dam. Contrary to the world expecting him to follow in daddy's cleats as a baseball player, our son's passion lies in WWE (World Wrestling Entertainment) as he studies acting.

His bedroom walls and shelves boast an impressive collection of various sports autographs which he's nabbed over the years, to name some: (baseball) Frank Thomas, Mariano Rivera, Wade Boggs, Eddie Murray and Mike Mussina; (wrestling) John Cena, Mick Foley, Kurt Angle and Jake "the Snake" Roberts; and (football) Ray Lewis. He sometimes drives to wrestler appearances laden with paraphernalia he'd like autographed, then returns home "pumped" that he owns a few more scribbles in his WWE coffee-table book *WWE Encyclopedia: The Definitive Guide to World Wrestling Entertainment,* written by YESNetwork.com editor Kevin Sullivan.

"Being face-to-face with wrestlers is very exciting," Dante said. "I feel like a little kid – I get giddy. Although, I feel very small compared to them, fame-wise and muscle-wise." He smiled and added, "Not so much in height though" as then he was shorter than Ken's 6-foot-4-inches but today just shy of it by half an inch.

Maybe someday Dante's collection might end up in a forgotten top-shelf shoebox like Ken's once-treasured baseball cards.

But I promised him I would never throw them away.

Dusting off a perfect game

It's not essential that I actually watch a Yankee game when Ken is home on an off day, since he treats me to the play-by-play from his favorite perch in the TV room. As he is "doing his homework" (how's that for an explanation of why a husband needs to watch so much baseball?), Ken calls out sporadically, "3-nothing Yankees!" ... or ... "CC Sabathia has a no-hitter going!" ... or whatever pinstripe action is unfolding on the screen. (He gets a little stirred up. Never met a man who loves baseball more than Ken.)

"What inning?" I called out about that particular game, knowing no player can count their baseball chicks before they hatch. Now, I don't exactly listen 100 percent to the baseball lingo floating around our house (being that it's daily), so I thought Ken meant CC was pitching a perfect game.

Later, when Ken's final game report echoed from the TV room that Sabathia gave up a hit in the eighth inning, I made a comment about a perfect game.

That's when Ken quizzed me. "Beauty," (he calls me that) "do you know the difference between a no-hitter and a perfect game?"

Although I could describe a perfect game (batters are up 1-2-3 and get out 1-2-3 for all innings), I failed the quiz by improperly describing a no-hitter, although I knew what I meant. (And how long have I been a baseball wife?).

I know what a perfect game definitely looks like, since I've been dusting a framed scorecard autographed by Dennis Martinez on display in Ken's office for 25 years. It's a keeper.

Okay, that's a white lie – I don't actually dust.

Martinez's perfect game July 28, 1991, is one of two that Ken has had the privilege of calling as an announcer — one in the National League and one in the American. That's some kind of baseball statistic right there since only 23 pitchers total have tossed perfect games in MLB history. The earliest two were recorded in 1880 and not another happened until 1964.

That perfect game between Montreal (2) and Los Angeles (0) was made sweeter for my husband to witness — and call — since Dennis is a former Orioles teammate, current friend, and a Montreal Expo starting pitcher during Ken's run at The Sports Network in Montreal, Canada.

Before YES Network evolved and Ken was a Yankees announcer on the MSG / (Madison Square Garden) Network, David Wells was the second pitcher to decorate Ken's office with a perfect scorecard May 17, 1998 (New York 4, Minnesota 0).

Super! Another dust collector … uh, I mean … keeper.

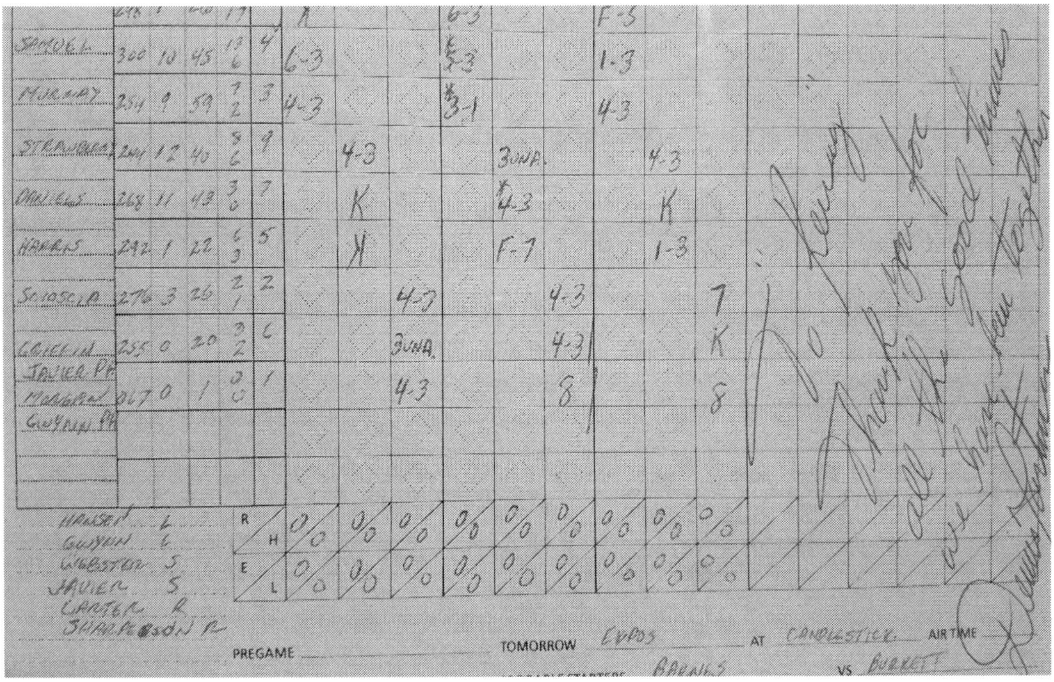

Ken's scorebook page kept during Expos ***Dennis Martinez's*** *perfect game July 28, 1991 vs. the L.A. Dodgers. As an Expos radio broadcaster, Ken had the pleasure of calling the game for his friend and former Orioles teammate. Dennis and Ken have remained friends throughout the years and participate in each other's charity golf tournaments. The scorecard is autographed by Dennis: "To Kenny, Thank you for all the good times we have had together." (Singleton photo)*

Please, no more chocolate cake!

Here's an oft-asked question: "What does Ken do in the offseason?" My common silly answer: "He bakes cakes."

Ken always makes up a funny reason to celebrate with cake. Daughter brought home straight A's? Ken baked a celebratory cake. Son received an acceptance letter from the college of his choice? Cake. TGIF? Cake. And the funniest excuse, after our daughter was donned in an actual NASA spacesuit at her high school during an astronaut visit, Ken baked a cake because "she returned from space."

And what do you know … there is actually an annual National Chocolate Cake Day and it's celebrated Jan. 27 in the U.S. – a day for those who love chocolate cake and other chocolatey goodies. What another ideal reason for Ken to pull out the electric mixer and a spatula. And he frosts them with *two* cans of icing, mind you, to ensure they are double-chocolatey. The man is a cake-eating machine.

Someone tell me how I'm supposed to shed extra pounds with all this cake in the house? I am forced to hold my nose to escape the tempting aroma for the 45 minutes a cake takes to bake. I don't wish to smell the sweet icing during his careful application lest I repeatedly dip a finger into the yummy container. (Because isn't the icing the best part? Ken leaves most of his on the plate, therefore, his double-frosting process perplexes me.)

Hurry up and get here, baseball season, so Ken can return to announcing and the oven is turned off. Not only because he needs to earn money to feed our family and stock the pantry with Pillsbury cake mixes; but also because he will be immersed in his favorite sport – the one he's forced to live without through the cold Maryland winter as the oven warms our kitchen.

Then he has his cake and eats it, too.

Ken's lifetime stadium pass

There's a metal gold and red stadium pass in our kitchen junk drawer about the size of a credit card. It reads: *American/National Major Leagues of Professional Baseball present this LIFETIME PASS to KENNETH SINGLETON AND ONE in appreciation of long and meritorious service.* It is signed by then-American League president Lee MacPhail Jr. and then National League president Charles S. Feeney (leagues no longer have presidents).

The pass is scratched up, bent, and tarnished – it's old – Ken retired from the field 32 years ago. While I was writing this, he saw the pass sitting nearby in my office. "I was looking for that," he said.

"You were?" I laughed. "Why? When would you ever need this?" Hard to imagine stadium personnel would require Ken to show his lifetime pass to get into any Major League ballpark as he works, nor does he attend games as a fan.

Besides sitting in the stands at Oriole Park at Camden Yards during Cal Ripken Jr.'s 2,131st consecutive game in 1995 (Ken had been invited to participate in a postgame ceremony), I've only seen my husband sitting in press boxes, not counting the bleachers at our three sons' Little League and Minor League games.

Wouldn't it be comical to see the look on a gate attendant's face if Ken tried to push through a turnstile using this metal pass? My guess is that no stadium staff has ever laid eyes on one.

"What *is* this antiquated thing?" s/he would ask. "Hold on, I better get my supervisor."

"I think once you play 10 years, you get one," Ken said. He cracks me up – he thinks he might use it "years from now." Guess I'll be the "AND ONE" he takes along.

Ken receives Lifetime Achievement in Sports award

Ken and I admittedly were greatly anticipating meeting actor Denzel Washington in March 2012 at the Rye Town Hilton in Rye Brook, N.Y., as hubby was slated to receive the Denzel Lifetime Achievement in Sports award from the Boys Club Girls Club (BCGC) of Mount Vernon. I admit, I felt such disappointment that Denzel didn't show up to host the gala (for reasons which event organizers did not say.)

Yet it turned out Ken was rewarded in more distinctive ways that evening than receiving a beautiful glass trophy or hobnobbing with Hollywood. He mingled and reacquainted with many of his childhood friends from his (and Denzel's) hometown of Mount Vernon – some of whom he hadn't seen since he left to play professional baseball. He was touched particularly when folks approached him to say they knew his parents, the late Joe and Lucille Singleton. "That made the whole night worthwhile," Ken said.

Actor Danny Glover and comedian JB Smoove provided the glitzy Hollywood component as they stepped on stage to stand in for Denzel. Learning about the mission of BCGC – and seeing so many alumni among the 600 guests – provided the inspiration.

"Our town was like the perfect place to grow up," Ken said. “It was a melting pot: one-third Jewish, one-third Italian and one-third black. People worked together. The schools were excellent, the recreation opportunities were wonderful, and it was close to New York City."

The mission of this national nonprofit organization is to fight juvenile delinquency by helping youth, especially those from high-risk neighborhoods, to make the most of their lives, with objectives to build self esteem, nurture talent and contribute to society on personal paths to success.

When Ken was growing up, the club was situated a half mile from the Singletons’ home on Seneca Avenue (sold to them by former Brooklyn Dodgers pitcher Ralph Branca). The BCGC was a facility that Ken and his brother Fred sometimes utilized as boys, a safe place in which to play in a weekend basketball league and socialize with neighborhood peers.

Decades later as it celebrated its 100-year anniversary in Mount Vernon, on South 6th Street, it offered even greater and more intricate programs and growth opportunities for kids than it did in the 1950s.

Comedian ***JB Smoove*** *jokes around with Ken at the annual gala of Boys Club Girls Club (BCGC) of Mount Vernon, N.Y., where Ken grew up. The organization awarded him its 2012 Lifetime Achievement in Sports award. (Photos courtesy BCGC of Mount Vernon)*

Little did the Mount Vernon BCGC founders know they would churn out Hollywood actors, professional athletes, entertainers, senators and a New York Yankees broadcaster. And little did the families of the young Mount Vernon children know they possessed the potential to grow into fine people who could achieve impressive careers.

"Every child follows a path in life," said Lowes Moore, executive director. "For many, that path will lead them to a door that gives them a place to grow, to learn, to belong, and a place to forge their future."

The following evening after the event, Ken, the kids and I had arrived home from New York. As I stopped to blow a kiss to my in-laws' smiling photograph, I thought about how much they would have enjoyed attending the gala. Not only because they were always very proud of Ken and Fred, but also to greet long ago friends and be in the area near where they had raised a family. The senior Singletons had set fine examples of how to make a life successful instead of wasteful.

For Ma and Pop Singy, the evening would have been superb – with or without Hollywood.

27 years is a whole bunch of baseball

By September, admittedly, I'm weary of baseball. Let's just get the Yankees to the World Series already, and get Mr. Singy home to make spaghetti. If I had a dollar for every baseball game I've watched (correction: sort of watched), I could have loads of fun at *The Dollar Tree*. (You thought I was going to say I'd be rich?)

Throughout Ken's radio announcing days for the Montreal Expos; TV broadcasting for Madison Square Garden and YES Network; son Justin's Little League, high school and Clemson University games; his summer leagues (including Cape Cod) and his Minor League career in the Toronto Blue Jays' Triple A system … wow, that's a *ton* of baseball for someone who identifies with the phrase *ants in her pants*.

Wait … I forgot to count two other sons' rec council baseball games; now we're up to over 25 years of being a baseball mom and wife, loyally sitting through mega-innings of a sport with which I maintain a love/hate relationship. (Good thing the tickets have been complimentary.)

It's not a secret – Ken admits it, too – baseball is a slow, methodical, and sometimes L-O-N-G game. I've been the one in the stands reading a book (a girl has to prepare for rain delays somehow), and I've walked around stadiums to stretch my legs and people watch. I've hunted for the healthiest stadium food possible and shopped in team stores to pass time through extra innings although our household doesn't need one more baseball jersey, cap or jacket in the closets. (Wait – do they make high heels with team logos?)

I try to pay attention, honestly I do, but the distractions are too great: watching people pig out and guzzle beer, noticing kids more bored than I am fiddling with their dad's hat or fold the stadium seat up and down 42 times. I contemplate why that girl walking up the aisle would show that much cleavage in a male-dominated venue (oh, right); and calculate the time we'll get back to the hotel to catch a *Sex & The City* rerun.

Basically, watching baseball is similar to accompanying my husband to work. The sport has been extremely good to the Singletons, certainly, I would never want to sound ungrateful (that's the *love* part). Baseball feeds our hungry kids – and my shoe fetish. Yet it separates our family for seven months (that's the *hate* part). We miss Ken, and he misses out on family life: birthdays, weddings, cookouts, cousins visiting from Italy, hanging out with the kids and other family events. We can bring his face into our living room via DirectTV, yet that is no substitute for the real deal.

Yes, 25 years is a bunch of baseball. Excuse me while I run out to the dollar store.

Ken was in the lineup

People ask often how Ken and I met, so I may as well share the story. How Suzanne and Ken ended up together is credited to my 8-to-5 corporate days as a communications officer for Maryland National Bank, where I was writer and editor of employee publications and coordinator of employee activities and trips. (It was a very fun job!)

After Ken retired as a player, he had signed on with the bank as a spokesman for a product called *The Lineup*, tied in neatly to a baseball theme. He made appearances at bank branches, taped a TV commercial with the late Clara Peller of "Where's the beef?" fame, and allowed our department to interview him for a 1985 issue of the bank's newspaper. I still have it.

I remember being somewhat nervous – excited actually – to meet a Baltimore Oriole on the morning he stepped into my lamp-lit office at 225 North Calvert Street in downtown Baltimore. Yet he quickly placed me at ease with his congeniality and handsome smile.

Ken had moved on to his second career, broadcasting games for TSN (The Sports Network) in Canada, which produced games for the Montreal Expos and the Toronto Blue Jays; he also anchored sports on the weekends for WJZ-13, a Baltimore television station.

"I enjoy it," he had said about being behind a microphone instead of at home plate. "I'm comfortable since I'm talking about something I've been doing my entire life."

On the topic of retiring from baseball, Ken explained during the interview: "There are different stages to an athlete's career. When you make it to the Majors, you make it on talent alone. You have the ability, but the talent and experience aren't mixed together. The longer you stay, the more the experience blends with the talent. In my case I was a good player, but I wasn't overly talented. As you get older, the talent decreases, then it gets to the point when the talent is almost gone and you rely solely on experience – which is not good enough. That's the point I reached."

The interview went on for a full page after that (how I wish I could edit my green writing!) with questions such as "What career would you have pursued if not baseball? (he said teaching); "Would you like to manage?" (no); "Who was your baseball idol?" (Willie Mays); and other topics.

Suzanne Molino & Ken Singleton *were married October 1991. Wedding guests included a few of Ken's former teammates and wives:* ***Ross Grimsley, Al Bumbry****, and the late* ***Mike Flanagan****. (Molino photo)*

Our Employee Communications department then began to produce news videos for the branches and satellite offices; Ken and I co-hosted those. I still have the videos, too, but I swear I'm not a packrat.

While sitting around waiting for the crew to set up shots, lighting, check sound and make script changes, Ken and I chatted off camera, and a friendship formed. Occasionally he would phone me at work, or we would meet downtown for a meal, still as friends. He was divorced, but I had a bow-tied banker boyfriend at the time – neither of us looked at the friendship as anything more.

After resigning from the bank in 1989, I freelanced as a communications and events specialist and was hired to help plan a treasure hunt fundraiser for the Cystic Fibrosis Foundation. The event called for local celebrities to present clues to the contestants, posted around various departments of Saks Fifth Avenue in Baltimore where the event was staged.

Ken had agreed to participate as a celebrity, and because my then-boyfriend chose not to attend, Ken and I went together. There was a magical kiss on the escalator at the end of the black-tie evening and later I broke up with the banker.

The next summer while I was renting a house with a roommate, the landlord decided to sell it. We approached our friend Ken with the idea to housesit for him while he announced Expos radio games; at that time, he worked every game, so he was on the road solidly from March to September. He agreed, and we moved in to what was supposed to be a temporary situation. At the end of that baseball season, my roommate left, I stayed, and the rest is history. We were married the following October in 1991.

And lived happily ever after married to baseball …

A sack of baseballs: Ken's autograph collection

When people and friends ask Ken for an autographed baseball (which is often), I kindly inform them that if they provide the item, Ken will be happy to sign it. We don't exactly own a warehouse of baseballs (see *The Singletons are fresh out of autograph items*). Of course, with nonprofit organizations and certain other stories that tug at my heart, I will scurry around the house in search of a blank baseball to stick under Ken's nose to sign.

There aren't many – blank ones, that is – so I buy a batch to have on hand to help nonprofits with their silent auctions. In Ken's office is a red felt, Santa-like bag filled with over 40 autographed baseballs. (I bought him a display case many Christmases ago yet it sits empty on the floor.)

Those baseballs – or rather what's on them – are impressive, even to my amateur eyes. I wish some of these guys had had better handwriting so I could better report the signatures on some of the balls; many are sloppily scribbled and thus illegible. Ken, without a doubt, could sit here and relay the stories behind each baseball in his collection. Here it is:

- Rawlings official ball of the 1983 World Series signed *"To Matthew, Good Luck, Pete Rose."* Unfortunately, Pete's scribble has a little company since our son Matthew, in a creative mood as a kid, decorated the ball using small rubber stamps;
- On another ball, Ken's handwriting reads: "RBI #100 and 101; 8/30/79 vs. Twins in Baltimore"
- On another: "1,000 Major League Hit, pitcher Jim Slaton, Milwaukee vs. Baltimore 7/25/77"

And others:

- "First A.L. Grand Slam 5/22/76, 8-4 win over Tigers"
- "1st American League home run, donated by Jim Perry 4/27/75"
- "Home run off Juan Marichal 6/13/71"
- "Home run #23, RBI #100, 9/23/73"
- "RBI #1000 & 1001, home run Chicago, 8/11/83"
- "9th Consecutive Hit, a club record, 4/28/81"
- "Career Home run #200, 4/26/81"
- "Hit #1,500 at Baltimore vs. Chicago, double, 1st inning, 8/6/80"
- "American & National 1979 Japan Major League Series"
- "N.Y. METS" with a ball full of faded autographs
- official league ball with Montreal Expos logo and various signatures

- "To Matthew & Justin, Al Bumbry, Padres #4, 1985"
- "50th All-Star Game" ball
- official ball of 1981 All-Star Game with various signatures
- baseball stamped with "Liga de Baseball Profesional de Puerto Rico"
- many other autographs too numerous to list; however, legible signatures include Frank Robinson, Earl Weaver, Eddie Murray, Cal Ripken Jr. and Jim Palmer
- A lone autographed ball with one signature sits amid Ken's baseball books on his desk; it reads Hank Aaron.

*Ken's collection of autographed baseballs includes these and one special ball that sits alone on his desk, signed by the great **Hank Aaron.***

The Singletons are fresh out of autograph items

I cannot envision the magnitude of fan mail and requests for autograph and auction items that must pour in for the extremely popular baseball players, not only to team offices, but to the players themselves.

Comparatively, Ken probably receives a smidgen of that amount as a former Major Leaguer; however, the requests still appear fast and furious – and he retired from the field in 1984. Not a week goes by that an auction item isn't solicited by a group or individual via e-mail, letter, phone, facebook, or verbally. And not a day passes that our Maryland mailbox doesn't contain fan letters mixed in with the junk mail. Three to five envelopes arrive daily from around the country from people requesting Ken's autograph.

We've given away autographed baseballs, bats, cleats, duffel bags, programs, scorebooks, baseball cards, postcards, lithographs, 8x10s, a stadium seat, posters, hats, personal photographs, and golf shirts ... you name it, Ken has signed it and I've mailed it. We've doled out these donations to schools, nonprofit organizations, dances, bull roasts, libraries, golf tournaments, Little Leagues, churches, baseball programs, and friends and neighbors ... for this cause, that cause, the best cause, the littlest cause, and for no cause at all.

Honestly, we're running out of items for Ken to sign. It's not like we stockpile an inventory of bats and balls in a warehouse attached to our house. The only items we buy and keep on hand for nonprofit organizations' silent auction requests are 8×10 photos of Ken swinging in an Orioles uniform and some baseballs. We still have a few aged pieces of O's memorabilia, such as programs and posters, yet not much that might draw big money in a silent auction.

As the unofficial administrative assistant to Ken Singleton, at times I've had to get creative when promising an auction item. I have created photo albums from our personal photos, such as a 2007 trek to Cooperstown, N.Y., for Tony Gwynn and Cal Ripken Jr.'s Hall of Fame induction (see Inside the Singletons' Photo Album). It included close-ups of Willie Mays, Yogi Berra, Brooks Robinson, and a bunch of other Hall of Famers. I wrote a handful of captions, included Ken's autograph, and the end result was a baseball decorated photo album that thrilled auction bidders.

Sometimes I stick under Ken's nose his used scorebooks to autograph, which I extract from a pile in his home office – those make great auction items. Filled with Ken's left-handed slant as he diligently keeps score during Yankees games while in the press box, one scorebook raked in $400 at a charity fundraiser. Nice!

And when I'm unable to locate any more big-ticket items around the house, I give away Ken himself! I create on the computer an attractive certificate for *A Round of Golf and Lunch with Ken Singleton*. Those have been popular, as Ken remains an admired sports celebrity in Baltimore.

So when the question is lobbed my way: "Does Ken have a baseball he could sign?" I suggest to autograph seekers that if they supply the ball, I will gladly ask him to sign it.

Notice I said, *I get the question*, rather than Ken; usually people are too chicken to approach him; just like in public. A fan may spot Ken, but s/he approaches me instead, "Do you think your husband would let me take his picture?" I redirect the anxious person in hubby's direction. "Ask him," I say. "He'll do it. And he doesn't bite."

If someone wants Ken's autograph badly enough, I figure they should be bold enough to ask him. But … they'd better find a piece of paper or pull a baseball out of thin air because, sorry fans, the Singletons are fresh out of autograph items.

Cows mooin' and taxis honkin'

Ken is always pleased to return to our Maryland home in the country after working in New York City, mostly because he sleeps better. We live in a small quiet town with one bank, one post office, one coffee house, deer galore and heaps of horse manure. When the windows are open in the evening, we can hear cows mooing in the far-off fields (not our cows!) and crickets chirping. The soothing stillness of the countryside rocks us to sleep like babies.

And not that we want to open a hotel window in Manhattan (nor is it possible – they're usually sealed), but city sounds are quite diverse compared to the country quiet. Instead of being lured to sleep, we lie awake listening to the blend of taxis honking, trash trucks beeping, sirens wailing, and those of you who are New Yorkers know the rest of the melodies. Cows not included.

New York City is an incredible town – we love its energy and resources. Ken was born in Manhattan and grew up in nearby Mount Vernon. He knows what to expect. "I'm back to my roots," he said.

One weekend when Ken had popped home before flying off to meet the Yankees in Detroit, I had invited him to sit on our front steps for a few minutes to watch the evening sky paint itself into a purple and orange combination. Here, in our small town, we are treated to stunning sunsets. And being that Ken had just spent almost two weeks in the city, he leaned over and said, "A little different than New York, huh?"

Because Ken works for the New York Yankees, people often ask why we don't live in The Big Apple. It is because we have the best of both towns: Manhattan with its wonderful perks and Baltimore County for its beautiful panoramas.

There's a time for New York City noise, and a time for stillness. And for the latter, there's no place like home.

Orioles magic restored in Memorial Stadium seat

We were thankful the water pipe in our club basement didn't burst over top of what I call “The Ken Singleton Shrine,” a wall of shelves holding cleats, photos, autographed books, trophies, plaques, a Memorial Stadium brick and other nifty memorabilia collected by and presented to Ken during his baseball career.

And we were extra grateful that the part of the basement floor that became sopping wet did not affect the Memorial Stadium seat I had gifted to Ken one Christmas. It's my favorite item in "The Shrine" – a treasured memento of Ken's 10 seasons in a great ballpark. This particular seat was once seat No. 29, same number as his jersey.

How many fans must have sat in this one seat over the years to root-root-root for the home team?

It's also a very good thing Ken wasn't with me in Baltimore the day in 2001 when I stopped by the dilapidated overgrown-with-weeds, half-torn-down Memorial Stadium on 33rd Street to retrieve the seat from a Maryland Stadium Authority rep. Ken may have cried – I almost did, pondering the many enjoyable spring and summer evenings and days attending Orioles games as a fan. How pitiful it was to see the death of the legendary stadium.

Because no matter what sort of new-and-improved, state-of-the-art, hoity-toity, high-tech facility the Orioles were building downtown, this was the famed Memorial Stadium on 33rd Street! The ballpark where countless great Orioles had pitched, batted, and fielded their way to baseball stardom. It was like watching an old friend take his last breath.

Memories surfaced of the days when one O's fan, “Wild Bill Hagy” (Section 34), bodily spelled out O-R-I-O-L-E-S regularly during each game; and when I had the delight of looking up at John Denver on the dugout stomping to the song *Thank God I'm a Country Boy* during a 1983 World Series game (almost a decade before I became Mrs. Singy). This legendary Orioles' seventh-inning stretch theme song still plays today at Oriole Park and was originally the idea of Dee Belanger, wife of the late shortstop Mark Belanger.

An artist friend, Linda Ports (who designed this book's cover) had been commissioned to refurbish and paint our ugly old gray stadium seat. After it was "dipped" to rid it of the many seasons of paint, Linda performed a little "Oriole magic" to bring it alive once again. She did a marvelous job on the project.

No one is allowed to sit in that seat, of course; it's slightly wobbly and probably wouldn't hold the weight. When we have parties, I run a piece of ribbon across it, in case a party guest is tempted to pretend s/he's cheering for the O's in Memorial Stadium.

I was given two stadium seats that day. The second one we had donated to a charity auction; it fetched a flattering $900. Not too shabby for a scruffy seat badly in need of an overhaul. Guess its Oriole magic was still intact.

(song of the era)

"Orioles Magic! Feel it happen!
O - R - I - O - L - E - S !

Magic! Magic! Magic! Magic!
Something magic happens, every time you go
You make the magic happen,
the magic of Orioles baseball …"

Tiny baseballs are painted on the studs of this refurbished Memorial Stadium seat from 33rd Street, which sits in the Singletons' club basement. Artist friend ***Linda Ports'*** *perfectly painted script captures the memories and marks the era. The seat was a Christmas gift for Ken from Suzanne. (Singleton photo)*

“Baseball teaches kids about teamwork – working for a common goal with peers … Sociability is also a big part of the game. Playing on a team is an opportunity for children to feel as if they belong to something.”

- **Ken Singleton**

9th INNING

Advice from the Pros

How to approach a player for an autograph

You spot him walking down the street like the average Joe, except his name is Cal, as in Cal Ripken Jr. You can't believe your good fortune in spotting a sports celebrity, or your chump luck that you're without a baseball. You nudge your kid, "See who's over there?" as you frantically search for a scrap of paper. You must act fast or he'll get away.

But how to grab Cal's attention? You want that autograph! Should you touch his arm? Call his name? Offer a handshake? A tongue-tied oaf with four thumbs stands in your place, confidence transformed, unable to contain his exhilaration in the same breathing space as a Hall of Famer.

Ripken said plenty of fans fumble their words out of nervousness. It amuses him when he hears, "You're my biggest fan," when someone means the opposite. Once he calms them with his gentle demeanor, they usually express themselves more clearly.

What's the best way to approach a player? Most people react without thinking, said Sandy Unitas, wife of the late Johnny U.

"We'd be sitting there [in a restaurant] and someone would obviously recognize him," Unitas said, "Then right when they served John his food, a fan would decide to approach him."

Her tip to the knack of celebrity approaching is to consider the situation. Where he is? How is he engaged?

"Wait until an approachable time," she said, "don't just run up and start talking, 'Oh my, he's Johnny Unitas!' and interrupt what's going on. Be considerate of the people he's with."

Unitas said her husband became a tad annoyed when a fan approached him during their kids' sporting events. "He was there as a father," she said, "not as a celebrity. He didn't like anyone talking to him while he was watching a game, including me!" One of the Unitas' sons, Chad, and our son Justin are friends from their days at St. Paul's School for Boys – kindergarten through 12th grade. Together, Ken and Johnny enjoyed watching the boys' basketball games.

Fans may claim the attention comes with the territory, yet any territory has its boundaries. And fans sometimes can cross the line ... such as when a hospital staff member asked Ken for an autograph while I was in labor.

Janice Murray, the former wife of retired Oriole Eddie Murray, once told me that so many stars and athletes are walking around the Los Angeles area, that most people don't give them the time of day. She said no one even bothered Eddie.

Yet one "how not to" incident stood out in her memory. As she and Eddie were leaving Dodger Stadium one day, a woman approached Eddie for a photo. "She shooed me out of the way," Janice said, "and said, 'Oh no, not you, honey.' That was kind of rude. There was a different way to do that. Maybe if the lady had been nicer, I would have offered to take the picture."

There are many good stories, too. "The kids were polite," she said, " 'Mr. Murray? Could I have your autograph, please?' That was no problem. Adults were the ones."

Autograph seekers should assess the situation, take into account the people the celebrity is with and the situation, i.e., is he or she rushing through the airport? Is it the appropriate time to interrupt them?

Brooks Robinson said 99 percent of the people he encounters are "wonderful" and respect his privacy. "I've always enjoyed people. I accept it; it's part of the deal." His wife, Connie, has patience with fans as well, he said.

Most are timid in approaching the third-base golden glover, yet he admitted an admirer occasionally might cross the line. "Sitting on the airplane, some guy wanted to bend my ear between Baltimore and Los Angeles. He wanted to talk and talk and talk and I couldn't get rid of him. Connie was with me."

Then there's the fan in the restaurant that talks for 20 minutes while the Robinsons were trying to eat. "That's crossing the line," he said. "But I've been around for so long, I can spot someone who wants an autograph. Some look at me and say, 'You're Johnny Unitas!' "

He shared Unitas' story about a guy in a bar who knew Unitas was an athlete, but was incorrect with the name. "You're Brooks Robinson," he insisted repeatedly. Unitas had to pull out his ID from his wallet to prove otherwise.

Teaching baseball to your kids: Tips from Ken Singleton

Baseball, hot dogs, apple pie and Chevrolet . . . remember that former car commercial jingle? Referred to a few all-American things that we love. We may eat an occasional hot dog, and some people know how to bake a juicy apple pie. And the majority of us know how to drive. Yet do we know baseball and how to teach it to our kids?

As a parent, taking an interest in America's favorite pastime and popular sport can be fun for you and your kids. Teaching and practicing baseball or softball with our youngsters can bring out the kid in us.

Baseball is more intricate than you might guess. It is a multifaceted game with countless rules, a sport that entertains many boys and girls.

Chances are, many of you played baseball or softball while growing up or carry fond memories of listening to the familiar stadium sounds on the radio with your parents on a hot summer evening. Maybe you're a parent experiencing your child's first year of T-ball, Little League or softball. Maybe you're a veteran of the game. Or, maybe you're totally baffled and uneducated about baseball because you may not be a regular fan.

For the love of the game, to spend quality family time together, or for whatever reason, let's get your youngster on her/his way . . . it's time to *Play Ball!*

Children often start with T-ball (age 4-6), in which the ball is not pitched but hit from a stationary position on top of a post. After T-ball age, coaches usually pitch to prevent games from running too long. Coaches also stand in the field to guide play and direct players where to run. Children begin to pitch solo generally in leagues for ages 9-10.

As a parent of a Little Leaguer, you may want to become involved in some capacity in the baseball/softball world. Certainly, you'll learn, too. Maybe you're unable to coach a team, but there are plenty of other volunteer opportunities. With hundreds of kids registered in ball programs, there's a need for umpires, managers, commissioners, team sponsors, coaches, equipment chairman and Opening Day coordinators.

Ken Singleton, who played in the major leagues for fifteen years, predominantly with the Baltimore Orioles, remembers as far back as age 4 learning the game from his dad Joe. Although he didn't play in an organized league until age 11, Singleton and his buddies played baseball in the playgrounds of his hometown, Mount Vernon, N.Y. He also played stickball and softball, and watched a great deal of baseball on television. "It was my favorite show," he says. Singleton has never left the game as he continues today in the press box broadcasting for the New York Yankees on YES Network.

Singleton's advice to parents is "not to expect too much early on. Remember your kid isn't Alex Rodriguez – yet." He reminds parents to have fun. "Try not to turn into an obnoxious Little League parent," he cautions. "Don't worry about winning and losing. Look for the improvement in your children even if they are the worst players. Don't become discouraged or feel embarrassed; your kids have plenty of time to learn baseball. It won't happen all at once." As your children's hand and eye coordination becomes better, they will improve, too.

Learning baseball is much more than developing skill. Baseball teaches kids about teamwork — working for a common goal with peers, whether that goal is getting three outs, making a double play or winning.

Sociability is also a big part of the game. Playing on a team is an opportunity for children to feel as if they belong to something. It's a chance to meet new friends and scoot the kids out of the house, especially away from addictive video games, other electronics and watching television.

Kids should understand that winning or losing is not the whole picture, although winning games can boost confidence. "No one ever appreciated winning until they lost a few times," Singleton says. When your child is upset about making a mistake such as striking out, he suggests naming a familiar player who also struck out in a recent game. "Professionals strike out, miss fly balls, get tagged out, pitch poorly and have hitless games, too," says Singleton. Kids can learn a lot from watching, so point out a particular player's style, such as a stance or swing.

Stress the importance of practice. As a youngster's skill improves, chances are the game will be more enjoyable; confidence will be elevated along with skill.

Getting started

- Show patience first and foremost. Remember how young and small your little player is.
- Practice with your child before registering for an organized team. This gives a sense of the sport instead of blindly sending a child onto the field.
- Play ball with your child as early as possible. Singleton started teaching his kids at age 2 (One son, Justin, caught the baseball bug and played from elementary school through high school, onto Clemson University and into Minor Leagues Triple A.)
- Show sensitivity to your child's moods. Be aware that some days kids aren't in the mood to play. Everyone has on and off days, even the pros.
- Interest in baseball should come from your child. Encouraging the sport is fine, but recognize and accept if your child would rather do another activity. Forcing a child to play a sport will result in frustration for both of you.

On swinging

- T-ball is effective; most kids can hit a ball this way. Kids who are new to the sport can become too discouraged trying to hit a pitched ball.
- Graduate your child to pitches as soon as possible to get the real feel of how baseball/softball is played.
- Start pitching with a big ball (such as a dodge ball) so your child can make contact. As proficiency is developed, decrease the size of the ball.
- Don't worry about form as much as enjoyment.
- Teach your kid not to be afraid of the ball by keeping both eyes on it. Point out the ability to control the ball. This applies to swinging and catching.
- Boost confidence by making the sport as easy as possible. Help your child to hit the ball by pitching slowly and easily.
- Use positive words versus pointing out errors and faults. Instead, show a better way. And certainly – no yelling or scolding!
- Be aware of the level of hand and eye coordination and practice accordingly.
- Provide the appropriate bat; start with a plastic one. It should be easy and comfortable for your child to swing (not too heavy or long). Go by "feel" when choosing, and remember the bat is for the child, not an adult.

- Switch-hitting (hitting left- and right-handed) can be practiced and learned at an early age. The earlier it is taught, the better and more natural it feels. Allow your youngster to try hitting from both sides if preferred, but do not force this.

On catching

- Provide a smaller baseball glove to fit a small hand.
- Roll the ball first, then graduate to a few bounces. Next, toss softly at close range.
- Remind your child to squeeze the ball after it lands in the glove and to trap it with the other hand.
- Most kids learn how to hit before they learn to catch. Kids are generally more afraid to catch a ball than to swing at one. Catching is harder to learn since kids feel they aren't in control of the ball approaching them.

During the game

- Be supportive and congratulatory. Offer tips in a positive way instead of pointing out mistakes or uneven skills. Because you are watching, your child will most likely want to do his/her very best.
- Support your child's interest with game attendance and enthusiasm. This is very important to a child! Being the only kid on the team whose parents aren't in the stands might make a child feel left out. If you or another parent cannot attend a game, maybe another family member can?
- You cannot teach *skill*. You can teach a child only how to apply what s/he has learned.
- If you are the parent *and* the coach, treat your kid the same as other players. This means no scolding, yelling and certainly no special treatment.

Off the field

- Watch baseball with your kids on television or listen to games on radio. Take your kids to Major League or minor league games or those at local high schools or colleges.
- Collect baseball cards to make the game more personal and interesting. As your kids learn who is on the field, they can identify with certain players.
- Watch a DVD on baseball instruction together.
- Register your kids in a summer baseball camp. Sometimes former players operate these, or they might visit the camp to offer tips and sign autographs.

The good thing about baseball and softball from a parent's perspective is that many parents have played the sport during their childhood.

"That's why fans think it's easy and tend to offer lots of advice from the stands," Singleton jokes. “But remember that not everyone is talented in baseball, so create a belief in your sons and daughters that they can learn to play well. More important than skill, type of bat or the rules, is the quality time you're afforded together as a family.”

EPILOGUE

And 10 makes a team

After fathering four children and being a grandpa to three, Ken Singleton finally has his own baseball team, including a Designated Hitter (DH) on the bench. Let's see how we would set up defensively on the field:

- Singy will be in right field since that's what he knew.
- Mrs. Singy will play shortstop since SS are her initials; it was her favorite position playing softball as a younger girl.
- Son Justin, formerly a Triple A minor leaguer, will take his former position at second base.
- His wife, Tricia, will be behind the plate as catcher; as a mom of three, she knows the importance of *home*.
- The six other Singleton kids and grandchildren will select their own positions, since as parents, we like to provide our kids with choices as they mature. We hope they choose to be in the right places and attract good teammates.

Mr. and Mrs. Singy will double their roles as manager and coach, because isn't that what parents and grandparents do? We coach our kids through life; show them what baselines to run and hope they move straight and forward. We trust they won't merely stand there and 'take' the pitch. We encourage them to swing for all they're worth. And if they miss – swing again!

If a fastball nicks them, we run over to ensure they are not hurt. We help our kids to stand upright and propel them back onto the field. We teach them the importance of good teamwork and camaraderie, and to gingerly field the plays in life in the best manner possible.

Should they make errors – and they will – they'll know this is normal and expected. There's always the next inning.

We cheer on our children to run fast and play hard. Various life skills will be taught and learned. We insist on *no spitting* on anyone and educate on preparedness as we send them out into the world armed with the proper protective equipment – and the best lessons taught to us by our parents.

Wear your uniforms proudly, kids. Handle your place in the lineup as best you can. And should you pop out, strike out or ground out, we're ready at the bench with a pat on the back and a "You'll get 'em next time." Losing games will teach you fine sportsmanship and to rise above defeat and scorn. And that tomorrow brings another game. Winning is a bonus.

Play ball. Play life. Play well.

Meet Mrs. Singy – Suzanne Molino Singleton

suzanne@SNIPPETSinspiration.com

Suzanne Molino Singleton's freelance writing career has produced numerous published pieces in magazines and newspapers around the country. As an official Major League Baseball blogger for the New York Yankees' YESnetwork.com between 2009 and 2013, Suzanne wrote *Mrs. Singy: Married to Baseball* from personal experiences, observances and milestone events in the baseball world, as the wife of former MLB pro Ken Singleton, Yankees TV broadcaster. She was a staff writer (2005-2009) for *The Catholic Review* newspaper, and has held various writing, marketing and public relations positions, mostly in the nonprofit sector.

Following a passion for her Italian heritage as the granddaughter of four Italian immigrants, this native Baltimorean is currently the pro bono director of the nonprofit organization, Promotion Center for Little Italy, Baltimore (promotioncenterforlittleitaly.org), which promotes the heritage, history and events of this charming ethnic neighborhood.

For 10 years as the creator of *SNIPPETS* Inspiration e-column, Suzanne continues to write this weekly reflective inspirational e-column that enjoys a loyal following. (Visit SNIPPETSinspiration.com to receive the free column via email.) Suzanne holds a Bachelor of Science degree in Mass Communications from Towson University, Maryland.

The Singletons have four children, a dog and three grandchildren, and reside in the country in Baltimore County where Mrs. Singy likes to bike.

Meet Singy – Ken Singleton

Nicknamed "Singy," Ken Singleton is in his 15th season as a New York Yankees analyst for YES Network, and periodically calls play-by-play. YES (Yankees Entertainment & Sports) is the exclusive local television station of the New York Yankees. Before joining YES, Singleton provided commentary on Yankees telecasts on the MSG Network (Madison Square Garden). In 1998, he was part of MSG's production team that won four New York Emmys for its Yankees coverage.

Ken also announced for The Sports Network (TSN) in Canada where he served as analyst for the Montreal Expos (1985-96). From 1991-96, he did play-by-play/analyst for CIQC Radio (Expos' flagship radio network). He was FOX Sports' lead analyst for its Saturday afternoon baseball broadcasts in 1996 and 1997.

Born in Manhattan and raised in nearby Mount Vernon, N.Y., Ken played baseball and basketball in high school, sometimes right across the street from the old Yankee Stadium. After receiving a *basketball* scholarship to Hofstra University, plus playing baseball there for one year, Ken was drafted by the New York Mets in 1967.

In 1972 he was traded to the Expos and in '74 to the Orioles. His .438 on-base percentage ('77); 118 walks ('75) and 35 switch-hit home runs ('79) established Orioles single-season records. Singy was named to the American League All-Star Team in 1977, '79 and '81. He was named Most Valuable Oriole in 1975, '77 and '79.

He received the Roberto Clemente Award in 1982 from Major League Baseball – the highest off-the-field honor in baseball. The award recognizes the player who best exemplifies the game of baseball, sportsmanship, community involvement and the individual's contribution to his team. Ken retired as a player after the 1984 baseball season as a three-time All-Star with a 1983 World Championship ring (Baltimore Orioles) and began his television career as a weekend sports anchor with WJZ TV-13 in Baltimore.

Currently on the Board of Directors for the Cool Kids Campaign that serves kids with cancer, Ken hosts the annual *Ken Singleton Celebrity Golf Classic* in Baltimore County, where he resides with his wife, Suzanne Molino Singleton (this book's author), their young adult children, and dog Razer. The Singletons are grandparents to three "little Singys."

Made in the USA
Middletown, DE
04 September 2016